From Roaring Boys to Dreaming Spires

Essays in Honor of John Wilson

Ron Rembert

University Press of America, Inc.
Lanham • New York • Oxford

Copyright © 1999 by
University Press of America,® Inc.
4720 Boston Way
Lanham, Maryland 20706

12 Hid's Copse Rd.
Cumnor Hill, Oxford OX2 9JJ

All rights reserved
Printed in the United States of America
British Library Cataloging in Publication Information Available

Library of Congress Cataloging-in-Publication Data

From roaring boys to dreaming spires : essays in honor of John
    Wilson / (edited by) Ron Rembert.
            p.   cm.
    Includes bibliographical references.
 1. Moral education. 2. Education—Philosophy. I. Wilson,
            John, II. Rembert, Ron.
    LC283.F76   1999   370'.1—dc21   99—36802 CIP

ISBN 0-7618-1482-5 (cloth: alk. ppr.)

♾™ The paper used in this publication meets the minimum
requirements of American National Standard for Information
Sciences—Permanence of Paper for Printed Library Materials,
                ANSI Z39.48—1984

Contents

Introduction   v
John Wilson's Major Publications   ix
Topics in the Top Ten by John Wilson   xiii

Introduction to Analytic Philosophy

Chapter One   Plato's Images Describing Discussants That Act Up and Discussions That Break Down
Ron B. Rembert, Wilmington College (USA)   3

The Basis of Moral Education

Chapter Two   The Basis of Moral Education
*Samuel M. Natale, Dowling College (USA)
and
Oxford University (England)
William O'Neill, Iona College (USA)
Joanne C. Neher, College of St. Scholastica (USA)*   19

Assessment and Practice of Moral Education

Chapter Three   The Context of Moral Education: The Virtues of a Learning Community
Felicity Fletcher-Campbell, National Foundation for Educational Research (NFER) (England)   33

Chapter Four   The Public School Model
*Henry Near, Oranim, Haifa University (Israel)
and
Oxford Centre for Hebrew Studies (England)*   45

Educational Research

Chapter Five   Being a Bit Pregnant: How
Philosophical Misconceptions Lead
to Stillborn Empirical Research
*Robin Barrow,
Simon Fraser University (Canada)*   63

The Basis of Education

Chapter Six   John Wilson and the Basis of Education
*Spencer J. Maxcy,
Louisiana State University (USA)*   85

Love and Personal Relationships

Chapter Seven   All You Need Is Love?
Charles Brock, Oxford University (England)   101

Response to the Contributors

Chapter Eight   A Personal Reply
John Wilson, Oxford University (England)   113

Introduction

In his book, *Reason and Morals* (1961), John Wilson anticipates a future connection between his early experiences at The King's School, Canterbury, and his later work in philosophy and education in the Department of Educational Studies, Oxford University:

There are times when philosophy needs to retire amidst dreaming spires: but there are other times when it needs to learn from roaring boys. (vii)

After serving "roaring boys" from 1953 – 1962 through various roles at The King's School, Canterbury (as a teacher of classical languages, history and philosophy and as a housemaster and deputy headmaster), John spent the next ten years on a journey leading him back to the "dreaming spires" of Oxford. Before returning to that setting of his undergraduate days, he accepted a position in Philosophy of Religion at Trinity College, Toronto, for the year, 1962 – 63, and in the School of Educational Studies at the University of Sussex for another two, 1963 – 65. At that point, John returned to Oxford and The Farmington Trust Research Unit where he extended his work in philosophy to the research field of moral education, 1965 – 1972. That assignment set the stage for John's appointment as Lecturer and Tutor in the Department of Educational Studies at Oxford University from 1972 – 1994 from which he moved into his current position as Senior Research Associate in that department.

While at Oxford, John Wilson has served as Fellow of Mansfield College, Research Consultant for the National Foundation for Educational Research (NFER), Editor of the *Oxford Review of Education*, President of The Philosophical Society of England, Research Supervisor of The Warborough Trust Research Unit, Chairman of the Oxford Philosophy Trust and Co-Director of the International Foundation for Religious Education, efforts making him nationally and internationally recognized in the fields of philosophy and education.

Introduction

His professional pilgrimage from Canterbury to Oxford took several interesting twists and turns, but, amidst the dreaming spires, John never forgot those days with the roaring boys. He returned to the university with its demands for research and analysis, but never lost sight of the practical and useful nature of his work. John believed, and still believes, that philosophy plays an important role in society, not just in the university. In his own words, John declares, "I see myself as more of a missionary than a scholar. My chief interest is in the interface between philosophy and practical affairs." His tireless effort to bridge the gap that can arise between town and gown, between theory and practice, inspires this collection of essays written in honor of John Wilson.

What better way to honor John Wilson than to involve him and the contributors in a discussion of topics in philosophy and education? Contributors to this volume testify to John's love of discussion, often referring in their essays to their own meaningful exchanges with him over the years. Those discussions continue in this volume with an examination of several topics covering the fields of philosophy and education.

In launching these discussions, John Wilson graciously agreed to list "Topics in the Top Ten" which he judges as important and about which he continues to write. This list provides an excellent overview of John's writing on a wide range of topics. It also serves as the starting point for the discussion between him and the contributors in this *festschrift*. The list of ten topics, along with John's commentary and questions regarding each one, serves as an invitation to our discussions with him in this volume, ones centering around research interests in philosophy and education he shares with the contributors.

The discussions start with the contributors addressing one of the ten topics, relating John's work to their own, in an essay. In a concluding essay, "A Personal Reply," John continues the discussion of each topic, noting his agreement and possible disagreement with the contributors. Through this special design for a *festschrift,* an ongoing discussion, we express our great appreciation for John's work and style, his encouragement of our work on these topics, and his abiding interest and willingness to continue our discussions with him into the future.

This collection of essays not only appraises accomplishments in the past, referring specifically to John Wilson's major work in the fields of philosophy and education, but also celebrates the present and future by

Introduction

continuing the discussion of various topics in these areas of study with him. A dynamic exchange emerges. The experience and talents of the contributors make such an exchange possible. I thank each contributor for sharing his or her own research in regard to one of the "Topics in the Top Ten" and, in the process, engaging John's work in that area. I also want to express special appreciation to John Wilson for his personal reply to the contributors. His response to the contributors adds a special touch to this volume.

I would also like to thank Dorothy Albritton of Majestic Wordsmith and Helen Hudson of the University Press of America for their special help in preparing this manuscript for publication. In addition, I would like to express my gratitude to David Johns and Mark Rembert for their technical assistance and to Theresa Rembert for her encouragement and support.

Ron Rembert, Editor

John Wilson's Major Publications
(Chronological Listing)

1956   *Language and the Pursuit of Truth*
               (Cambridge University Press)

1958   *Language and Christian Belief*
               (MacMillan)

1958   *The Truth of Religion*
               (S.P.C.K.)

—

1961   *Philosophy and Religion*
               (Oxford University Press)

1961   *Reason and Morals*
               (Cambridge University Press)

1962   *Public Schools and Private Practice*
               (Allen and Unwin)

1963   *Thinking With Concepts*
               (Cambridge University Press)

1965   *Logic and Sexual Morality*
               (Penguin Books)

1966   *Equality*
               (Hutchinson)

1968   *Introduction to Moral Education*
               With Williams, Sugarman
               (Penguin Books)

John Wilson's Major Publications

1968 *Philosophy*
(Heinemann)

1968 *Education and the Concept of Mental Health*
(Routledge)

1969 *Moral Education and the Curriculum*
(Permagon)

—

1970 *Moral Thinking*
(Heinemann)

1971 *Education in Religion and the Emotions*
(Heinemann)

1972 *Practical Methods of Moral Education*
(Heinemann)

1972 *Religion*
(Heinemann)

1972 *Philosophy and Educational Research*
(National Foundation for Educational Research)

1973 *The Assessment of Morality*
(National Foundation for Educational Research)

1973 *A Teacher's Guide to Moral Education*
(Chapman/Cassell)

1975 *Educational Research and the Preparation of Teachers*
(National Foundation for Educational Research)

1977 *Philosophy and Practical Education*
(Routledge)

John Wilson's Major Publications

1978 *Preface to the Philosophy of Education*
(Routledge)

1979 *Fantasy and Common Sense in Education*
(Martin Robertson, Oxford)

—

1980 *Love, Sex and Feminism*
(Praeger)

1981 *Discipline and Moral Education*
(National Foundation for Educational Research)

1983 *Dialogues on Moral Education*
With Barbara Cowell
(Religious Education Press)

1983 *Philosophizing About Education*, (ed)
With Roger Straughan
(Holt, Rinehart, Winston)

1986 *Violence and Vandalism*
(J. Howson, Oxford)

1987 *Philosophers on Education*
With Roger Straughan
(MacMillan)

1988 *A Preface to Morality*
(Macmillan)

1989 *Taking Education Seriously*
With Barbara Cowell
(Althouse Press)

—

John Wilson's Major Publications

1990   *Children and Discipline: A Teacher's Guide*
        (Cassell)

1990   *A New Introduction to Moral Education*
        (Cassell)

1990   *Central Issues in Moral and Ethical Education*
        With Samuel M. Natale
        (University Press of America)

1993   *Reflection and Practice: Teacher Education
        and the Teaching Profession*
        (Althouse Press)

1995   *Love Between Equals*
        (MacMillan)

Topics in the Top Ten
by
John Wilson

(Editor's Note: To promote discussion as the basic design for this *festschrift*, John Wilson graciously agreed to identify *ten* general topics or areas about which he has written and continues to write, one or more of which connects with each contributor's particular interests. Under each topic, he offers some comments about his own work in the area and provides questions as starting points for further discussion.)

(1) Introduction to Analytic Philosophy

I have written three works on this topic, and am not really happy about any of them. *Thinking With Concepts* concentrates on the particular skills and techniques of conceptual analysis; *Language and the Pursuit of Truth* is more systematic, taking the reader through the different types of words, statements and meaning; *Philosophy* is more informal, illustrating the analytic approach to particular problems (justice, art, democracy, etc.). How exactly people ought to be introduced to this kind of philosophy stills seems to be an open question and a rather important one.

Questions: Under what conditions is analytic philosophy best taught and learned?
What kind of psychological resistance to it should be expected, and how can that resistance be overcome?

(2) The Nature and Force of Analytic Philosophy

Partly from my dissatisfaction with these introductions, but chiefly because many people seem to misconstrue the nature and power of analytic philosophy, I tried to explore this topic more deeply in *What Philosophy Can Do*. I argue in that work that analytic philosophy has much more practical weight and relevance than its own practitioners often suppose. I also try to explain something of the resistance to it which is commonly felt. There is much more to be thought and said about this last point (something which I want to investigate more fully in my declining years).

Question: Can analytic philosophy give us a substantive knowledge about what is true or what is valuable?

(3) The Basis of Moral Education

I spent some years on this topic and produced the not very satisfactory *Introduction to Moral Education* about thirty years ago. The more recent *New Introduction to Moral Education* is a distinct improvement. I owe an enormous amount here to R.M. Hare in advancing the thesis that morality is a form of thought and that moral education involves initiation into that form, rather than proceeding from a predefined moral content.

Question: Can moral education rest solely on pure reason and logic, or must it start by assuming a particular moral content?

(4) Assessment and Practice of Moral Education

With slightly more originality, I attempted in *The Assessment of Morality* to draw a full and clear list of the components, attributes and mental equipment which I took to be relevant to moral thought and action and to take the first steps in clarifying how their presence or absence might be assessed in various individuals. In *Practical Methods of Moral Education*, I also described four or five methods that seemed logically necessary for such education and that could be easily adopted in more or less any educational establishment.

Question: What structural or other changes in schools are needed to make them more effective for moral education?

(5) Religion and Religious Education

Because of the connection of morality with religious and other ideals, I was led in *Education in Religion and the Emotions* to work along lines parallel to # 3 and # 4 above. It seemed to me that reason gets a grip on religion and quasi-religious ideals chiefly through education of the emotions: it is the appropriateness of our attitudes, particularly the attitude involved in worship, to certain religious objects that is in question, not any kind of empirical or super-empirical facts.

Questions: In what way is religion within the scope of reason? What basis could there be for education *in,* not just *about,* religion?

(6) Educational Research

As an educational researcher and teacher-educator, I tried in *Philosophy and Educational Research* to show the necessity of analytic philosophy in the first stages of any serious educational research, something still largely absent in our own day, following this up by a number of articles in educational research journals. Other works, especially *Fantasy and Common Sense in Education,* reflect the same interest.

Questions: How important is philosophy for educational research? What educational changes are needed to bring philosophy to bear more effectively?

(7) Teacher-Education

I made two efforts at this, the first in *Educational Theory and the Preparation of Teachers* and more recently in *Reflection and Practice*. In these works, I challenged the idea of any respectable corpus of 'educational theory' and the currently fashionable idea of teachers as mere 'apprentices' who should acquire a number of 'skills' purely by 'practical experience'. My view continues to be that teachers should be educated primarily in philosophical and psychological analysis or psychotherapy.

Question: What should be the core disciplines or most essential types of learning in teacher-education?

Topics in the Top Ten

(8) Discipline and Authority

I singled out this particular area in education because of my belief that educators, at least in liberal or pluralistic societies, had lost their grasp on these basic concepts because of a quasi-paranoid feeling against the exercise of *impersonal* authority and the use of punishment. That concern emerged in a partly empirical research project written up in *Discipline and Moral Education*. Philosophical points are also discussed in *Philosophy and Practical Education* and in *Children and Discipline*.

Question: What kind of discipline and authority should educators be able to deploy in schools?

(9) The Basis of Education

I attempted in *A Preface to the Philosophy of Education* to lay the philosophical groundwork for education by analyzing the concept marked by 'educate' and 'education', considering the nature of learning and laying out some options for the curriculum in terms of what kind of knowledge might be seen as especially valuable. Like the rest of my work, this piece was based solely on conceptual analysis rather than ideological persuasion or intuition.

Questions: Do we have a value-free concept marked by 'education'? If so, what ground does that concept cover?

(10) Love and Personal Relationships

I became interested in this area partly because I came to see philosophy as a form of friendship or a kind of personal relationship. That realization led me into this whole area marked by 'love', 'sex', 'sharing the self', 'communication', 'trust' and other such ideas. I completed two works, *Love, Sex and Feminism* and *The Logic of Sexual Morality*, both rather light-hearted in tone. I recently published *Love Between Equals*, a more serious work. I see such love as a kind of unity, a seamless web which can unite both some of the ideas about *eros* in Plato's *Symposium* and what Aristotle says about intrinsic friendship in the *Nicomachean Ethics* (*philia*). In this book, I advocate such love as a form of life to be preferred to the more altruistic or self-sacrificial ideal of charity or *agape*.

Question: Are there various kinds of love between equals, or only one kind?

Introduction to
Analytic Philosophy

Chapter One

Plato's Images Describing Discussants That Act Up and Discussions That Break Down

Ron B. Rembert

My interest and work on the so-called Socratic Method of teaching led me to visit Oxford and John Wilson in 1978. I have vivid memories of my first meeting with him. A young, American graduate student, I arrived at his office at the Department of Educational Studies, ready to introduce myself, chat and enjoy a cup of tea. To my surprise and eventual delight, Wilson bypassed the pleasantries and launched us immediately into a discussion on that occasion. Later I came to realize that this was John's style on most occasions: discussion, first; tea later (although many discussions took place during tea time in the Common Room). My first impression was that I had walked into the setting of a modern Platonic dialogue, with all the hopes and fears associated with such a possibility, facing someone like Socrates himself. Not so much because of his way of *doing philosophy*, although John's incessant questioning and insightful responses reminded me in many ways of the ancient Greek philosopher, but much more because of his genuine interest and concern about *teaching others to do philosophy*. From the outset, Wilson's philosophical skills dazzled me, but his pedagogical convictions inspired me. The same was true of Socrates, whose concerns as a teacher I had grown to appreciate as much as his interests as a philosopher.

Wilson's insights about teaching grew more impressive with my reading of his published works, especially those where he talks specifically about the struggles to face and the pitfalls to overcome in *doing philosophy* and in *teaching others to do philosophy*. For example, in one of his earliest works, *Thinking With Concepts*, a primer introducing conceptual analysis, Wilson devotes an entire section to consideration of "difficulties of temperament" in doing such analysis (1969: 16). His short list of "psychological obstacles or resistances" which may arise in pursuing it include (1969: 16 – 20):

1. The feeling of being hopelessly lost
2. The feeling that questions of concept can be settled much more easily than in fact is the case
3. A curious compulsion to analyse everything
4. The inability or unwillingness to talk or debate, either with oneself or in discussion with others
5. A superficial fluency which impedes rather than assists the flow of thought, by obscuring it with a flow of words
6. The desire to moralize

In a later piece, *Dialogues on Moral Education*, a light-hearted treatment of a serious topic written in the form of a Platonic dialogue, he again addresses at some length the pitfalls which can lead to a breakdown of discussions. In this instance, a discussion falters from the outset because the two potential discussants, a father and a son, adopt different perspectives which undermine their exchange. The father assumes an 'authoritarian' position about morality, making the activity of discussion appear unnecessary to the son. (1983: 20 – 21) Why discuss a question for which there is only one answer, especially if that answer is already known? The son posits a 'relativist' position about the matter, making the activity of discussion appear irrelevant to his father. (1983: 22 – 23) Why discuss a question for which there are so many possible answers, all equally correct, depending upon one's opinions? Socrates strives to help these two potential discussants avoid the pitfalls created by these two opposing stances, neither of which makes discussion possible or plausible. In this instance, he is as involved in teaching them how to do philosophy as in doing it himself. These two works serve as examples of Wilson's attentiveness, as a philosopher and as a teacher, to what inhibits analysis or disables discussion.

Two questions, how do discussants act out? and why do discussions break down?, arise from these works and appear to intrigue Wilson as much as they do Plato. Wilson's fascination with such questions about what *does not* work, especially in the more affective domain as discussants engage in discussions, ignites my own interest in this area. And, like Wilson, I appreciate the use of Plato's dialogues as helpful sources for pursuing these questions. It might appear more practical to turn to the disciplines of psychology or sociology as sources for exploring these issues, and, indeed, those disciplines provide many insights about these matters. However, Plato's dialogues serve as unique sources. They have an unfamiliar and a familiar ring, including images that are ancient, yet contemporary, in meaning and use. Using them as interpretive devices for exploring the problems and prospects of 'discussion' in Plato's dialogues and in current classrooms stands as the goal of this essay.

Plato's Dialogues

In his dialogues, Plato employs vivid images in describing discussants who act up and discussions that break down. These images surface here and there in Plato's texts. Their random appearance does not draw much attention to these images, certainly not the kind of attention they deserve. Taken as a group, however, they prove impressive. In addition to enhancing the literary quality of Plato's texts, they provide us with a useful vocabulary for describing what discussants *should not do* and how discussions *should not proceed* to be successful. In other words, the lessons offered through these images are negative in tone, describing what one ought not to do, in promoting meaningful and productive philosophical analysis and discussion. Describing what not to do proves as important, if not more important, than describing what to do.

A partial list of Plato's images describing discussants that act out and discussions that break down follows:

Discussants That Act Up

— a discussant who acts like "a stone sitting beside me, a real millstone with neither ears nor brains" (*Hippias Major* 292d)
— a discussant who acts "like books, they cannot either answer or ask a question on their own account" (*Protagoras* 329a)
— a discussant who acts "like a gong which booms when you strike it and goes on until you lay a hand on it" (*Protagoras* 329a)
— a discussant who "shaking out every reef and running before the wind, launching out on a sea of words till he is out of sight of land" (*Protagoras* 338a)
— a discussant who acts "as someone [who] pulls a stool away when someone is going to sit down" (*Euthydemus* 278b/c)
— a discussant whose actions "sew up the mouths of people" (*Euthydemus* 303d/e)
— a discussant who acts "like wild boars charging against the spear thrust" (*Euthydemus* 294d)
— a discussant who acts "like a foal, young and flighty" (*Gorgias* 482c)
— a discussant who acts "as a poet might quarrel with an actor who spoiled his poems in reciting them" (*Charmides* 162c/d)
— a discussant who acts like "a wild beast, he hurled himself upon us as if to tear us to pieces" (*Republic* 336b)

Discussions That Break Down

— discussions reach a point "like children [chasing] after larks" (*Euthydemus* 291b))
— discussions reach a point "like falling into a labyrinth" (*Euthydemus* 291b)
— discussions reach a point "like tossing on the waves of argument, and at the last gasp" (*Laches* 194c)
— discussions reach a point "as if with lying men" (*Lysis* 218d)

Take the image of "a stone sitting beside me, a real millstone with neither ears nor brains," for example. Plato uses this image in describing a discussant in his *Hippias Major* (292d). Socrates introduces this image during an imaginary dialogue with himself offered for Hippias' sake. It is apparent that this image of the "stone" refers to Hippias, however camou-flaged by the imaginary nature of Socrates' monologue. The critic in the imaginary dialogue, represented by Socrates, criticizes his imaginary discussant, representing Hippias, for not listening closely or thinking seriously about the definition of 'beauty', the actual discussion topic. For example, notes Socrates, when asked by the critic, "What is beauty?," the imaginary discussant simply lists beautiful objects, from young maidens to wooden ladles, as possible answers (287e – 291b). Such answers reflect a lack of attention to the demands of that question, responds the critic. Thus, acting as an imaginary critic, Socrates proceeds to describe Hippias, his imaginary discussant, as "a stone sitting beside me, a real millstone with neither ears nor brains." But the negative lesson about how not to act as a discussant transcends the imaginary dramatization. If Socrates and Hippias are going to proceed with their discussion, rather than face a possible breakdown at this point, Hippias cannot continue to act like "a real millstone, with neither ears or brains." He will have to intensify his attention, and offer answers appropriate to the question under consideration.

Imagine looking at a person sitting next to you during a discussion and thinking to yourself, "that person is like a stone sitting beside me, neither listening or thinking about the topic." Or consider someone thinking that way about you. Would it prove helpful to use such an image in describing one another? Using Plato's image *during* a discussion to describe each other's behavior might create more problems than it resolves. After all, even Socrates employs it in an imaginary setting, making the point more indirectly, rather than confronting Hippias directly with the criticism. Might it prove more productive to remind all discussants of this possible behavior, which needs to be avoided, at the *beginning* of a discussion? Using Plato's image in this manner might involve making an agreement at the outset, such as "let's agree that, as discussants, we won't allow each other to act like 'a stone sitting', neither listening closely nor thinking seriously about the topic, because, if we do, the discussion will break down." I propose that this use of Plato's images at the outset to clarify expectations of what discussants *should not do* during the discussion would prove helpful. Even more, once expectations have been set by learning from the images at the start, employing them during the discussion would serve as a reminder of what to do, rather than a negative putdown of what not to do. With this approach, the images serve both as a set of expectations to pursue and as reminders of behaviors to avoid, signaling potential ways in which discussants act up and discussions break down.

Examining these images in their contexts in Plato's dialogues serves as a starting point for retrieving the advice contained in each one. Each image needs and deserves much more exploration than the following brief commentaries provide. These first glances at the images are intended as invitations to deeper reflection and richer interpretations.

Plato's Images Describing Discussants That Act Up

Other images from Plato's dialogues beside (1) "a stone sitting beside me, a real millstone with neither ears nor brains," pinpoint actions discussants should avoid during discussions. For example, another reminder about *how not to act* follows:

(2) A discussant who acts "like books, they cannot either answer or ask a question on their own account" (*Protagoras* 329a)

In discussions with rhetoricians such as Protagoras and his students, Socrates often draws a distinction between making speeches and engaging in discussion. Training in speechmaking does not prepare rhetoricians to be effective critics during a discussion, notes Socrates. Speaking eloquently involves different skills than those required for discussion, especially those employed in analyzing one's own or other's views about a topic. "Like books," speech givers present words, but cannot always engage in a critical discussion of them. They speak as though guided by a prepared script, one which may or may not even reflect their own ideas. This tendency to rely on a planned presentation often inhibits the speechmaker in asking or answering questions throughout the exchange, an expectation of discussants which rhetoricians are not prepared to meet.

(3) A discussant who acts "like a gong which booms out when you strike it and goes on until you lay a hand on it" (*Protagoras* 329a)

(4) A discussant who "shaking out every reef and running before the wind, launching out on a sea of words till he is out of sight of land" (*Protagoras* 338a)

Again, Socrates employs these two images while drawing a distinction between making speeches and engaging in discussion. However, he pinpoints a different kind of problem in this set than in the previous image. Perhaps some rhetoricians, while being well trained in giving speeches, also acquired the ability to ask and answer questions, skills not developed by those who simply act "like books." Nevertheless, in displaying this ability, they may tend to dominate the exchange, especially with fanciful talk, as they are trained to do. "Like a gong," they talk endlessly without self-restraint or they find themselves "launching out on a sea of words . . ." before they realize the impact. This tendency keeps the speech giver from serving as an effective listener during a discussion, one who can engage and then disengage from one's own view when appropriate.

(5) a discussant who acts "as someone [who] pulls a stool away when someone is going to sit down . . ." (*Euthydemus* 278b/c)

In his discussions with eristics such as Euthydemus, Socrates raises questions about the multiple meanings of words. Knowledge of a range of meanings, especially of key concepts, proves invaluable during a discussion. However, using such knowledge to confuse the discussion, rather than to clarify it, undermines the activity. Shifting from one meaning to another unexpectedly can leave other discussants bewildered or disoriented. "As someone [who] pulls a stool away when someone is going to sit down" tricks the unsuspecting victim, a discussant who deliberately shifts meanings of words without warning tricks others. This tendency to play tricks with language keeps one from serving the important role of word analyst during a discussion, one who diligently questions language use and misuse.

(6) A discussant whose use of words "sew up the mouths of people." (*Euthydemus* 303d/e)

In his discussion with Euthydemus, Socrates also raises the issue of common meanings and typical distinctions associated with various words. Words, especially concepts, may cover a range of meanings, but one generally accepted meaning usually works during conversations or discussions. Deviating from this meaning in an unusual or ridiculous way simply for effect or show can leave others speechless. Playing with the meanings of words has its place, but does not usually help to promote discussions. As if intended to "sew up the mouths of people," blatant misuse of words, even for the sheer fun of it, can make ordinary communication practically impossible. This tendency to play with language at inappropriate times in unhelpful ways keeps oneself, rather than the discussion, at the center of attention, making one's contribution a source of distraction which inhibits, rather than promotes, the participation of others.

(7) A discussant who acts "like wild boars charging against the spear thrust" (*Euthydemus* 294d)

In a discussion with Euthydemus, Dionysodorus and Ctesippus, Socrates offers this image to describe an inclination to boldly answer every question put forth during a discussion, claiming to know answers which one does not know. Answering questions stands as an important goal during a discussion, but determining which questions need to be answered and what kind of answers are required by questions, involves the discussants in self-evaluation. They must face the limitations of their knowledge, recognizing the range of what they know and do not know. Otherwise, "like wild boars charging against the spear thrust," these unreflective discussants will pursue questions which might be irrelevant or accept answers which might be mistaken. In either case, this tendency to answer any and all questions during a discussion keeps one engaged, but in a potentially unreflective way, making one's contribution a possible impediment, rather than an aid, to the exchange.

(8) A discussant who acts "like a foal, young and flighty" (*Gorgias* 482c)

In his discussion with Gorgias and his student, Polus, Socrates offers this image to describe Polus' propensity to make assumptions about Socrates' views before the philosopher has an opportunity to clarify them. Discussants face many temptations such as this during a discussion, allowing their own thinking to anticipate, overrun or outrun, the thinking of others. The ebb and flow of a discussion heightens this temptation because discussants, especially eager ones, think ahead and beyond the present exchange in formulating what might be said in reply. "Like a foal, young and flighty," they lack the self-control and discipline required in seeking clarity and precision from point to point. This tendency to preempt another's contribution can keep one enveloped in one's own flights of fancy, unattentive to the thinking of others or the course of the discussion.

(9) A discussant who acts "as a poet might quarrel with an actor who spoiled his lines in reciting them" (*Charmides* 162c/d)

In a discussion with Socrates about the definition of 'temperance', the young Charmides offers a definition learned from Critias, but one for which the young student does not want to argue strongly. Before assuming responsibility for his own view and offering an argument in support of it, Critias criticizes Charmides for lacking understanding of it. The older Critias allows the younger Charmides to speak for him, but then chastises him for not speaking well. "As a poet might quarrel with an actor who spoiled his lines in reciting them," a discussant who allows another to speak in his behalf runs the risk of misrepresentation. The remedy comes not from chastisement, but from assuming responsibility for one's own views. This tendency to allow others to assume such responsibility keeps one partially involved, but detached, and open to misunderstanding by others.

(10) A discussant who acts "like a wild beast, he hurled himself upon us as if he would tear us to pieces" (*Republic* 336b)

In a discussion with Polemarchus, Socrates interjects this image to describe the dramatic entrance of a bystander, Thrasymachus, to their exchange. Without warning, Thrasymachus launches into a personal attack on Polemarchus and Socrates, accusing them of giving into one another without much critical evaluation as they express their views. Attacking the person during a discussion usually inhibits, rather than enhances, the activity, forcing the discussants in response to defend themselves more than their positions. Under these circumstances, emotions reign while thinking wanes. Like persons confronted by "a wild beast," discussants may grow more fearful, anxious and distracted by such personal attacks. This tendency to interject personal attacks into a discussion keeps one preoccupied with the personal level of interaction, making it difficult at times to distinguish between the persons and positions presented.

These ten images from Plato's dialogues draw attention to a variety of ways discussants might *act out* during a discussion. These images are not the only ones appearing in Plato's works, but they serve as examples of the rich collection of images found there, ones which can help us realize and recall certain behaviors on the part of discussants which lead to the breakdown of discussions.

Plato's Images Describing Discussions That Break Down

Other images in Plato's dialogues describe moments at which discussions appear to *break down*. These images shift our focus from behaviors of individuals to behaviors of groups. Like the images listed above, this set provide lessons of what *does not* work, what needs to be avoided in regard to interaction in a group, to keep discussion from breaking down.

(11) Discussions reach a point "like children [chasing] after larks" (*Euthydemus* 291b)

For Socrates, this image captures a moment of frustration in trying to reach a conclusion that remains slightly beyond the support of the evidence. Reaching conclusions stands as an important goal of a discussion, one which provides some motivation for engaging in the activity. After all, if the activity involves little more than sharing opinions or exchanging views, without hope of a potential conclusion to be reached in the end, the purpose for participating in it diminishes. However, if the goal to reach a conclusion outruns the means for achieving it, that is, the collecting of sound evidence, the formulating of strong arguments, the analysis of language use and misuse, etc., then the discussion may grow frustrating, "like children [chasing] after larks," wanting to catch what is close at hand, but what remains just out of reach.

(12) Discussions reach a point "like falling into a labyrinth" (*Euthydemus* 291b)

For Socrates, this image expresses a sense of futility arising from going around in circles during a discussion, thinking that the end is near, only to find that the search has drawn the discussants back to the starting point. Discussions do not always follow straight lines. They often branch out in various directions. However, "like falling into a labyrinth," discussions can grow so convoluted and confused that the discussants lose all sense of direction in their inquiry. A sense of helplessness can arise, leaving the discussants with little confidence about choosing what questions to ask, what answers to pursue, what ideas to discard, what suggestions to follow. The activity of discussion may grow more debilitating than enlivening at this point, if the discussants are unable to curb the spiraling effect they are experiencing.

(13) Discussions reach a point like "tossing on the waves of argument, and at the last gasp" (*Laches* 194c)

For Socrates, this image serves as a way of encouraging Nicias, a bystander, to enter a discussion between Socrates and Laches, one which is floundering. At this point in their exchange, Laches appears to lack the endurance and perseverance required to continue the search for a definition of 'courage', a concept which may appear easy to define at first glance, but which presents several difficulties to Socrates and Laches. Discussants need endurance and perseverance in discussions of difficult topics, especially those focusing on the definitions of concepts. "Tossing on the waves of argument" can grow tiresome, leading discussants to that feeling of "the last gasp" unless someone can help the drowning victims to catch their breath, renew their energy and regain their focus on the discussion topic.

(14) Discussions reach a point "as if with lying men" (*Lysis* 218d)

For Socrates, this image serves as a note of caution that the excitement and anticipation to reach a conclusion during a discussion may prematurely convince the discussants that a conclusion has been reached. In a discussion about the definition of 'friendship', what appears to be a sound conclusion about the definition of that concept to the excitable Lysis and Hippothales turns out not to be in Socrates' view. In the young discussants' fury to reach some agreement and in their desire to please themselves, Socrates realizes that the boys may be deceiving themselves about the soundness of their conclusion. Monitoring *how* carefully one is arguing, not just *what* one is arguing, remains a constant challenge to discussants during a discussion. Without such vigilant oversight, they treat each other no better than "lying men," disregarding issues of clarity and coherence for easy answers and faulty conclusions.

Applying these Images to Improve Discussions

These images from Plato's dialogues might remind us of problems with discussants and pitfalls during discussions with which we are already familiar.

How Discussants Act Up

— Not participating (Image #1)
— Making speeches, not asking/answering questions (Image #2)
— Answering questions by making speeches (Images #3,4)
— Playing with words (Images #5,6)
— Answering any and every question, regardless of importance (Image #7)
— Claiming to know more than one knows (Image #7)
— Jumping to conclusions (Image #8)
— Attacking other discussants (Images #9,10)

How Discussions Break Down

— Desiring to jump to conclusions without enough evidence (Image #11)
— Going around in circles (Image #12)
— Lacking endurance, perseverance to tackle difficult topics (Image #13)
— Overlooking faculty reasoning (Image #14)

Although we are familiar with these problems and their possible consequences, we may not prepare ourselves as discussants at the beginning of discussions to anticipate and avoid them. How many discussions start with any review of ways discussants should and should not act or how discussions proceed, when productive, and how they do not, when unproductive? If no review occurs, then like the discussants in Plato's dialogues, we may be poorly prepared to address these issues before they arise. We may assume that familiarity with discussion means awareness, that past experience translates into future insight, but those assumptions may lead us into the same problems and pitfalls that faced Socrates and his discussants in Plato's dialogues.

Might not Plato's images serve as a useful resource for preparing ourselves from the outset to anticipate and avoid these potential problems and pitfalls? Specifically, might not they serve as helpful reminders of how discussants *should not act* and how discussions *should not proceed*?

Interpreting each image would serve as the starting point. Are discussants aware of the type of behavior that the image, for example, "like a gong which booms when you strike it and goes on until you lay a hand on it," describes? Have they experienced such behavior, on their own or other's parts, during a discussion? Is it clear why this is a behavior which detracts from, rather than enhances, discussion? After interpreting the image and recognizing it as describing a problem to be anticipated and avoided, discussants would set up the expectation that they should not act "like a gong which booms when you strike it and goes on until you lay a hand on it." If anyone begins to act this way, they should expect a reminder not to do it. This use of the image carries a literary charge, an emotional punch, which might prove more effective as a deterrent during a discussion than simply reminding discussants not to make speeches or dominate the exchange. If discussants agree to accept this expectation about what not to do from the outset, then a hint from each other during a discussion that "you're sounding like a gong" might curb that tendency. Without having established it, such a reminder would probably sound comical, at best, or insulting, at worst, and prove unproductive in allaying inappropriate behavior.

As another example, take the image of "falling into a labyrinth." Again, from the outset, if discussants reminded each other that this sensation serves as a warning that the discussion may be breaking down, then they should be in a better position to heed the signal and avoid this pitfall. This image, like the others, serves as a dramatic cue to a potential problem that isn't usually described in these terms. Using these terms can have an empowering effect, enabling discussants to monitor the progress of their exchange on various levels, anticipating and, perhaps, avoiding an unproductive line of inquiry. If the discussants could agree from the outset that they will try to take seriously that sensation of "falling into a labyrinth" and utilize it as a warning that discussion may be breaking down, then they might also anticipate and avoid this potential pitfall.

Plato's images, drawn from sources rooted in a different time and place, are familiar enough to apply to our own understanding of ourselves as discussants engaged in discussions. They are even translatable into terms we currently use in describing ourselves along these lines. Yet, these images remain unfamiliar enough to challenge continuously our interpretive skills. Their literary quality protects them from simple translation from one context to another. These images challenge us to make sense of them, and, in so doing, come to understand ourselves. Expressing lessons that are universal without losing their sense of particularity, these images from Plato's dialogues remind us of the unending effort to define the discourse needed for understanding ourselves, especially as discussants who tend to act up during discussions that break down.

The Basis of
Moral Education

Chapter Two

The Basis of Moral Education

Samuel M. Natale, William O'Neill and Joanne C. Neher

Moral education can, and certainly should, rest on reason and logic. That, however, does not necessarily entail that having particular moral content, even at the start, conflicts with a foundation in reason and logic. In some types of thinking, reason and logic are inherently involved with content and with experience, such as occurs when natural logic is applied. This term would be difficult here to define or describe precisely, but rather can be understood by saying something like (in a moral sense): "Do not lie," "Do not injure others," "Do not take what is not yours," etc. Natural logic may be considered holophrastically as early elements in moral reasoning which can be borne out relatively directly and easily in experience. This could be either in terms of the consequences of these acts in the ways situations work out or in terms of the way people react to you when they find that you have disregarded or violated one of these principles. There are other than moral senses in which we can see the same kind of logic occurring. Principles about thrift, cleanliness, being prepared, promptness, taking steps to remind yourself of things you must not forget, etc., can also be adduced and be given contexts in which they would be naturally reinforced or borne out.

Another sense of natural logic has to do with simple sentences and observational terms, an issue which is rather technical, epistemologically speaking, for this discussion. Perhaps it is enough to add to the above that a fundamental and natural logic involves some basic sense of what an argument is. Also, notions such as deduction from general rules to individual instances and induction to rules from accumulated instances. Logic can, of course, be studied and practiced to the point of being endlessly technical and sophisticated.

To reprise, we may propose that moral education requires, obviously and absolutely, the capacity of reasoning and must involve an initial and ongoing attention to developing, for a child or older student, the ability for clear and critical thinking and reflection. Both children and older students, however, must be given, in the form of initial direction, some basic concrete norms. These will be appropriated and adapted through a process of adjustment in the course of personal experience and verified through the understanding of their real consequences. What are the bases, conceptually, for looking at moral education in this way? What are the implications and evidence psychologically?

If we consider the notion of practical knowledge, traditionally spoken of as practical intellect, we can discern that there is a formal structure to such knowledge which makes it different from systems of abstract knowledge or of explanatory thinking. Such abstract knowledge, whether in the case of a science or of metaphysics or of mathematics, etc., has a basic structure after it is acquired. That structure consists, first, of general principles and, then, the deduction of more narrow and particular principles from these. In the explanatory phase, it involves the interpretation of particular instances or cases in terms of the principles so derived. From the point of view of a methodology, we rediscover some process of proposing a hypothesis to be tested against some carefully articulated, and perhaps frequently revised, criteria of truth. The forming of the principles, as well as their application to the interpretation of individual instances, constitutes knowledge.

Science, in this sense of knowledge, involves technically precise and clearly agreed upon canons of what constitutes evidence that would confirm or disconfirm some hypothesis. Also, scientific thinking would involve technically precise and agreed upon canons of how data are to be gathered and interpreted, how measurement is to be done, and how advanced mathematics will be introduced for calculations. Conclusions arrived at in these ways will involve a canonical method and will be logically arranged from the most general laws, through more particular principles, to individual instances to be explained or understood.

The methods of attaining principles, understanding their implications, and revising them in the light of disconfirming evidence, clearly require a foundation in logic and reasoning. One might wish to call this pure reason in the sense that it must, to a large extent, be accomplished in advance in order to be able to say that one actually knows something as a result of experience and application.

Children very likely begin to understand such areas of knowledge by being given some content in the form of particular principles or of results of testing and other confirming experience. Developmentally and chronologically, learning of this kind may proceed in this way. But, logically, one must at some later time come to an understanding of the processes of forming principles, deducing from them, applying them, and testing their applications in order to be able to say that one understands things and, therefore, truly knows them.

The paradigm involved in this way of schematizing the structure of knowledge is traditionally thought of as having as its objective the acquisition of something denominative as 'truth', if not absolutely conceived, then pragmatically grasped. It is essentially knowledge 'of' something. Such knowledge, of course, is capable of being turned toward another objective: knowledge 'of how to do' something. Technical and practical applications of otherwise abstract or 'objectively true' knowledge follow in this order. Skill can be acquired and cultivated in consequence. This brings us again to the consideration of another type of knowledge traditionally considered as practical knowledge or, perhaps, as the use of practical intellect or practical reason.

This reason has traditionally been thought of as the function of practical intellect or of the mind functioning in a practical way. That is, practical reason is the aspect of reason aimed not at acquiring theoretical or factual knowledge, nor at forming concepts or conclusions in a purely abstract way, but rather aimed at doing something. It is reasoning about action, and the object of the reasoning and of the action are the same thing. Learning the principles of leadership, for example, is aimed at learning how to prompt people successfully to cooperate or organize their efforts toward some goal. That objective is not to know certain abstract truths or facts, but to be able to achieve such results with actual people when the occasion arises. The same may be said about the principles of salesmanship as instruments of practical reason. Sometimes the distinction has been made between, on the one hand, a sort of pure practical reason or a set of highly generalized practical principles and, on the other hand, applied practical reason in the concrete. Whether so fine a distinction is needed at the outset of moral education is dubious.

Moral reasoning can be distinguished from other types of practical reason in a couple of important ways. One way is that moral reasoning is practical reasoning about that which is highest or most important or, traditionally, most excellent in the order of action or accomplishment. To be morally good is the highest, most important, and most excellent of purposes. Another distinction is that moral reasoning can be, in at least some cases, categorical or unqualified. One might argue that one should study hard if one wishes to get good grades in class or that one should work quickly if one wishes to finish the job on time. But these are not moral senses of 'should'. One might say categorically or unqualifiedly that one should not lie or that one should not steal. Period.

Moral education and moral thinking are further distinguishable from the more general category of practical knowledge. Abstract principles of logic are, in a sense, immature at the start of moral education. To be sure, modal logic and moral reasoning patterns are important and may have a priority in the logical order, but they are not prior in the chronological (developmental) or real order of learning. The reason that such abstract principles are, in a sense, immature at the beginning of the process of education is because the principles and the judgments are practical rather than theoretical or purely abstract.

A further advance upon this notion, particularly important to the discussion as applicable to educational concerns, might be seen in the famous discussion in the eighth book of Aristotle's *Nicomachaean Ethics*. Among other topics, Aristotle discusses some fundamental components of the notion of community. He observes that the most important things that people may hold in common or upon which they may base their friendship or love are what we might call their shared values. In Aristotle's way of putting it, the greatest thing people might hold in common is their sense of what is just.

In learning of morality and in the development of the moral skills or virtues, the source and the object of the lesson are the same. Moral principles in the concrete are learned from and true of the same experiential occasions. The experiences which give meaning to the acts of moral judgment are the substance of moral knowledge and also its purpose.

The process of moral education does not principally have an object acquired within itself. The object of this knowledge lies in doing things. Acts and words are the finality of virtue and moral judgment.

The place of abstract moral logic is at the more mature point of the learning process where the ability of making moral judgments is already considerable cultivated. At this stage abstract reflection may have the advantageous effect of helping a person to reach greater clarity about moral choice and judgment. Prior to this, the development of recognition and responsibility are the principal points of focus.

Recognition here refers to the process of learning how to see and know moral elements, moral moments, and moral choices in the concrete. It consists of the actual situational awareness of the moral importance of a choice that faces one and the importance of the link between one's choices and the potential outcomes. Recognition involves the sense, not only of what should be done reasonably or even logically, but of the worth or higher value of doing it.

Responsibility here refers to seeing something as flowing actually from one's deeds and one's decision. Still more profoundly, responsibility refers to my understanding the decision and outcome in a particular situation as coming from one's character with its strengths and weaknesses. The skills of moral judgment as currently developed and as, perhaps, needing to be enhanced or refined are a part of what is known and understood in the concrete case of applying and interpreting moral principles with whatever moral content is subscribed. It is not simply a question of what should or should not be done, but of what can be done specifically with me as actor and with my judgments and character as instrumental.

The purpose of moral education or learning is not, as in other cases, the acquisition of abstract knowledge. It is not even simply the cultivation of the ability to turn abstract knowledge to practical action. Beyond knowledge and application, moral learning implies understanding of oneself and one's nature, understanding what constitutes a good life, a life worth living, and the ability to establish it as a genuinely possible goal.

When moral education has succeeded to the level of such significant understanding, the possibility of another type of abstract knowledge emerges. This type is moral theory. In this area of moral education or learning, the point is to reflect critically and analytically. Such reflection is appropriately abstract and is focused on the meaning of moral values and the nature of moral character and judgment in relation to higher ends.

If wisdom is considered as a goal or object of moral learning and practice, then it should be fairly clear that the abstract in the order of such an education comes at a later developed phase of that education. Wisdom, which is inherently concrete, ultimately facilitates the development of abstract moral logic and of moral theory.

To summarize: moral education cannot rest solely on abstract principles nor upon pure logic. It can be founded in part upon these, but this is only to speak in the logical order in which principles are prior to application. In the real order, the chronological order of learning and of education, the principles of morality are constituted of practice and terminate in practice. In due course of the process of moral learning, when it is well advanced, algorithms of modal logic and patterns of moral reasoning can be studied and used to shed light on further practice.

One does start by assuming some particular moral content. By this is meant taking up initially and provisionally some fundamental moral norms that can be rendered meaningful as they are tested, personally appropriated, and refined in concrete experience. It should be understood that assuming some particular moral content in this way does not mean taking it for granted or accepting it as established beyond questioning or criticism. Assuming some particular moral content more simply means proposing it to initiate the process of learning. The substance of moral learning, the knowledge gained itself, includes most essentially the knowledge of oneself as an instrument and an effective actor to the extent that one has or lacks the skills of moral judgment and choice.

Expansion of the Model

Beyond the clear contribution that Wilson's model makes to the whole range of moral analysis and action, thorny problems of both research and implementation remain. Probably the least developed aspect of the model of moral education centers around the general preconditions necessary for the possibility of effective, efficient action coupled with understanding and developmental movement.

In the earlier portion of this chapter we referred to the necessity that moral content be tested and explored in experience and in analytical reflection upon experience. These abilities require consideration of components that are essentially psychological, sociological, educational and cultural at a minimum.

While reason and logic as the foundation of moral thinking are appealing, many other components are critical, not the least of which is the emotional security of the person as actor. Clinical and developmental literature charts the transitions, reactions, adaptations and sense of mastery that form our emotional security. In some sense, all of these must be in place at a "good enough" level to permit a person to make unconstrained decisions and to implement these into action. Experience and reflection are never static, but remain a process which results in both autoplastic and alloplastic adaptations of the actor.

All of the above requires consideration of values, needs and expectations. While it is possible to offer some training in ground rules, the internalization of these will require experimentation, exploration, intuition and, of course, failure as well as success. By success, we mean an action essentially understood as necessary and acted out with the explicit understanding that the needs of others enjoy the same status as one's own.

Nor can the problem of language be passed over in silence. The development of linguistic skills appears central to conceptual understanding. This is increasingly problematic in a global environment where it appears much of what we have taken as universal of a *datum* is, in fact, simply a cultural expectation or norm. The necessity of separating universal concerns and, as it were, 'rules' from cultural norms requires rigorous examination conceptually and, we believe, empirical exploration of how decisions which are termed 'moral' are made and implemented. The advance of pluralism within global unity is more than linguistically interesting. With one world interacting more closely than ever before in history, the collisions between varied value systems and the moral education which arises from them is more intensely obvious.

Tied directly to these concerns is the person's ability emotionally or affectively to relate to other people. That is, the person's ability to perceive others as thinking, feeling creatures with the same requirements for dignity, equity, etc. is crucial.

Finally, of course, the social structure of the family, schools, community, country and globe becomes a necessary consideration for moral education. Like it or not, our social experiences form and constrain and/or intensify our vision of what is expected from self, others and the society at large.

Commentary on the Model

From a purely developmental perspective, there is one facet of the basis of moral education that has not been discussed. The psychological, sociological, educational and cultural abilities mentioned above are essential. In addition, there is an underlying set of tools brought to any educational experience, the basic physical ability to learn and grow, the biologically-based ability to integrate any knowledge, including the abstractions of reason and logic. If this is not in place, there will be great difficulty in achieving a level of moral reasoning necessitated in any society. However, once this biological structure is in place, from heredity and environment, the groundwork is laid for the absorption of content reflected in moral education. Throughout the preceding essay, there are references to development, to the need for experience as a tool to shape and be shaped by moral principles. This development is facilitated by access to the resources needed for physical growth and maturation. That *access* to resources is based on culture and environment.

If the resources are in place for learning, then the focus can shift to that learning which begins through experience. From experience the person begins to form a worldview that is both unique to the individual and shaped by that person's environment. Moral education is a part of that experience, absorbed first in the microcosm of a dyad, usually mother-child, then the family, then expanding into formal educational environments and finally into adulthood where a higher level of abstraction can be attained in moral reasoning.

Two assumptions have already been made in this section. First, there must be a biological readiness for learning. Social theorists call this a 'critical period', where the human is best prepared and most ready to absorb new material. For example, a child who does not learn to walk within the first year or two of life will have a more difficult time learning this later. The child is most receptive to internalizing this skill in infancy. Another example is someone who does not learn to read during the early years of education; this person will find the development of reading skills much more difficult in adulthood.

In the area of moral education and moral theory, there are also critical periods, times when the person is more open to internalizing the concepts needed to behave in a moral way. Wilson states that moral principles are learned *from* and are true *of* the same experiential occasions. The critical period for development of a moral framework is much broader than the two examples given above. The critical period for development of this framework is, in some ways, life-long. The person usually begins to learn early in life—some theorists maintain this is pre-birth—and this learning begins to shape the adult view of morality. The primary concepts of right and wrong are learned repeatedly during a person's existence. As more and more experiences become internalized, these experiences are used to refine constantly the moral framework used in decision-making. The power of experience must be considered in how it affects the person. The key is to be receptive to the moral learning that can shape behavior.

Wilson states that people must understand themselves and their unique natures. This understanding provides the person with a groundwork for approaching the world, the social structures of dyads, as well as the structures of family, schools, community, country and globe that Natale discusses. This understanding is also coupled with decisions, based on moral learning, that shape what constitutes a good life, a life worth living, and the ability to establish it as a genuinely possible goal. One very significant difficulty arises from this perspective, however. This difficulty is referred to by Natale as the social experiences that form and constrain and/or intensify our vision of what is expected from self, others, the society at large.

Moral reasoning is an end and a process towards which the person strives. The question immediately arises as to which ends are 'best', which are 'acceptable', and which are 'right' and 'wrong' for the person. These issues are more easily addressed within the smaller systems of people's lives, i.e., dyads, families and possibly neighborhoods. Once the person becomes involved in the larger community, through education, employment and independence, the questions about ends and processes become blurred by the multicultural aspects affecting modern social structures. As Natale states, language is bound by culture, which, in turn, affects decisions about behavior. Are moral decisions global, considering widely varied perspectives, or are they based on cultural norms and expectations? Are they situation-based? This question will be set aside for later comment. If there must be a basic moral theory that guides as well as is guided by behavior, is this theory culture-bound? If so, is there any possibility that a concept of moral education can even be discussed, when that education is shaped by culture?

This question leads into the comments made by Natale about the consideration of values, attitudes, needs and expectations. Theorists from many perspectives will agree that these concepts exist in all cultures.

But when any moral theory is applied to these, when moral decisions are based on these, there can be immediate repercussions that can be either positive or negative. When there is agreement on the decision, that it "fits" the norms and expectations of the culture, or seems to be the best answer in a particular situation, it most likely will be seen as based on moral reasoning. Of course, the opposite may be true when the decision is seen as not fitting the culture.

It is clear throughout this essay that there is a dialectic component to moral education and moral reasoning. Decisions are shaped by moral logic; moral logic in turn shapes decisions. From the individual's earliest experiences with 'right and wrong' behavior, through refined behaviors well into adulthood, there is a constant flow of energy between the development of moral reasoning and the outcome of it, i.e., behavior. Wilson discusses wisdom as the goal and object of moral learning and practice. Wisdom is seen as concrete, learned through positive and negative experiences. Wisdom is gained through the development of skills related to emotional security, the concept discussed by Natale. People grow and develop through trial and error, even if they have listened to instruction from others. This trial and error is the groundwork for the development of wisdom, forming a person's individual worldview and behavior patterns. Wisdom is *practical*, translated into the everyday interactions of people in their environments, assisting people in having access to various resources.

These interactions are then processed by the individual, and either confirm or confuse the moral stance of the person. From a human behavioral perspective, this process is defined as *neuro-linguistic programming*. This has three components. The first is the nervous system through which experience from all five senses is received and processed. Second is nonverbal communication, allowing for coding, ordering and assigning meaning to experiences. The third, programming, is directly related to moral reasoning. It provides for the ability to organize the other two components, the nervous system and communication, in ways that achieve desired outcomes. Desired outcomes equal thinking and behavior, designed by the ability to internalize and organize experiences, and then to act in and react to the environment. Therefore, wisdom can develop from these practical experiences.

Wilson maintains that people begin their moral development by assuming some particular moral content. To expand on this, the concept of neuro-linguistic programming must be understood in how it affects this content. Once there is some grounding in a perspective on moral content, the person is able to test and refine decisions, based on continual rethinking of moral theory, as expansion of experiences lends itself to this testing and refinement. Again, the dialectic of actions-theory-actions is present. From this development of a moral perspective comes responsibility for one's actions. The flow from deed to decision that Wilson discusses, which comes from a person's character, is directly affected by strengths and weaknesses brought to that flow.

Tying all three sets of comments together, the implication is that there must be a biological predisposition present for learning to take place. This predisposition allows for trial and error, and the development of emotional security within the person's environment. This emotional security, based on cultural norms and expectations, becomes the tool for development and implementation of sound moral reasoning. The question remains as to whether this reasoning can be global when the concepts of a multicultural environment are addressed. The provision of a beginning moral framework from which to work may only confuse the issue in a global environment. Any framework is culture-bound. Therefore, any moral decisions affecting education or behavior must be tested and questioned within that culture.

Application to a broader environment may not be practical or useful. And, although the idea that moral education can rest on reason and logic is true, the critical thinking expected of students must be enhanced by an understanding of how their outcomes of thinking and behavior affect and are affected by environmental experiences. Logic skills mature along with the students, providing the tools necessary to be a moral thinker, applying reason to decisions and developing theory from the consequences of those decisions. Then, the immaturity involving abstract principles of logic at the start of moral education, discussed by Wilson, will be reduced. The student will begin to mature in thinking, reasoning and behavior as abstract principles of moral education become integrated into the student's moral perspective through testing and refinement.

Assessment and Practice of Moral Education

Chapter Three
℘⊗
The Context of Moral Education: The Virtues of a Learning Community

Felicity Fletcher-Campbell

It is a source of amazement to me that John Wilson's seminal work delineating the components of the morally educated person (1972a) has been so neglected by those working in the field of moral education. The challenge of criticism and of debate about the soundness of the typology has been avoided. This is both disappointing, not least to Wilson who is one of the most 'public' of philosophers and always ready to engage in open dialogue about what he has proposed, and surprising. Wilson's model does at least give a framework for schools to plan the curriculum and offers a serious, possibly unique, attempt to lay down the attributes, skills and knowledge that need developing to facilitate the emergence of a morally educated person.

Essentially, the model delineates the 'end product'. There is a set of issues relating to this end product which the model, *per se*, does not address. First, it does not discuss the balance between the components, either in the course of acquisition (and there is inevitable disequilibrium in the process of learning most things) or at the point of acquisition.

Second, it does not consider the 'degrees' of mastery or acquisition (for example, within a Kohlbergian framework, the components might look rather different, or appear in various guises at different stages). Third, in itself, it does not prescribe a methodology insofar as this is logically dependent on the set of components. Whereas Wilson does not really address the first two points elsewhere in his writings, the third he does, and it is that point which I shall consider in this essay.

In *Practical Methods of Moral Education,* Wilson asserts that

> The intelligent reader, if asked whether moral education should be done by 'academic' methods (classroom periods) or 'social' arrangements (creating a 'good' atmosphere in the school), would dismiss the question as silly. He would say, rightly, we need both. (Wilson, 1972b, p. 93)

He goes on to point out the complexity of the interrelationship between the social and the academic, and states that they cannot be dissociated. First, learning in each context has to be made explicit. There has to be "cross-referencing" and "ways must be found of getting the pupils to put together the various contexts" (p. 99) so that development of the moral components is nurtured. Second, organisational and pedagogic methods must be derived from the moral components insofar as these arrangements must ensure or facilitate the development of those components: debate about 'in-class discussions' or the tutor system, for example, must not be grounded in ideologies which are not informed by the moral components. Third, any social arrangements in the school must be necessary preconditions for moral education: certain pupil/teacher relationships, for example, may lead to different outcomes; the deciding factor about where they are adopted is the extent to which they contribute to moral learning.

Wilson believes that the connections are best exposed in a potent social context in which the pupil can feel secure and be emotionally committed. At the time of writing, Wilson considered this context best exemplified by the traditional English public (independent) school, itself having many parallels with what was considered a 'standard' family at that time. Such an institution, he felt, offered a meeting place for the 'academic' and 'social' contexts and provided opportunities, not only for the application of theory but also, *pari passu,* the theoretical examination of dilemmas arising within communal living.

Rereading parts of *Practical Methods of Moral Education* nearly twenty-five years after it was first published, it is tempting to dismiss the material as 'dated'. Approaching the millennium from a UK perspective, accusations could be made that it is ethnocentric, sexist, elitist and culturally alien. Wilson's distinction between the classroom and social life outside it, but within the institution as a whole, is important. It harmonizes with descriptions of the 'total' life of the school as articulated in school brochures, including 'extra-curricular' activities or, rather, 'the whole curriculum', if one understands 'the curriculum' to be all the structured activities in which a young person engages at school. But his model was strongly influenced by the male, academically oriented, public school regimes existing in England in the 1970s. These regimes have themselves changed radically, propelled by other social changes in the past couple of decades. Furthermore, such institutions educate only about seven per cent of the relevant school age population in England and Wales. Opportunities for social life in the state-maintained day schools in which the vast majority (about 93 percent) of young people in England and Wales are educated are considerably more restricted than in Wilson's proposed model. Many schools, for example, report a decline in out-of-classroom activities such as sports teams and clubs, largely on account of teacher workload occasioned by externally imposed curricular, organisational change and reduction in resources.

Thus the sort of set-up advocated by Wilson seems increasingly nebulous and inviable within the present context of education. Notwithstanding any evaluation of its effectiveness or the cogency of its logic, the model is harder to apply as we approach the millennium, purely for practical, socially informed reasons. Is the implication of this, then, that moral education, as articulated by Wilson, suffers in the light of these external restrictions or can we find some other way of showing the connectedness?

I suggest that the interconnectedness between social and academic contexts, which Wilson identifies as necessary, can be prompted in a way different from the one which Wilson advocates, a way which is more securely grounded in why a school, essentially, exists and which Wilson argues for elsewhere (1977). It seems to me that the moral virtues and components flow from or can be cultivated by the intellectual virtues, broadly understood, which are imperative for fostering learning and the attitudes necessary for a 'learning society'. The intellectual virtues are themselves 'moral' and can serve moral education. As the *sui generis* function of the school, *qua* institution, is to educate or to bring about learning, even if by default other functions largely due to social welfare have accrued to it, then it must surely be desirable to maximise what attaches to or flows from this core function, rather than to set up opportunities for parallel, discrete functions, in this case, social arrangements for moral education. This, in essence, accords with what, I think, Wilson was saying. He was not advocating separate systems, but drawing attention to the unity of the whole way of life he describes. The way of life was already existing and was one with which he was fully conversant, having had considerable experience, both as pupil (scholar at Winchester) and teacher (second master at King's Canterbury) and, no less, as student (scholar at New College) and tutor (fellow at Mansfield College), the ethos of the Oxford college being within the same tradition. The fact that Wilson may have, apparently uncritically, accepted this way of life is neither here nor there in terms of those features of it that he chose to highlight, and which served his purpose at the time.

What I shall propose is that the connectedness which Wilson rightly considered important can be maintained by focusing on the quintessential features of schools which he identifies elsewhere, but does not make explicit when he discusses particular social arrangements.

In order to discuss this connectedness, we must have some idea of what a school is, *qua* institution, that is, labelled as 'school' as opposed to another institution offering something to young people. After all, schools are not in place solely to promote moral learning. Hypothetically, the latter might be effected partially or entirely by other, purely social arrangements, provided that the means of developing Wilson's GIG or the mastery of factual knowledge were present in a structured way. No, schools exist to develop a range of intelligences (Gardner, 1993) and ways of investigating and coming to terms with the world. Essentially, most of this effort comes under what we broadly understand as the formal curricular divisions of maths, history, science and so forth.

Articulating the dispositions required to engage in education, Wilson (1979:74) wrote of the way in which:

> an average person has to put himself—that is, his natural desires and impulses and interests—in the background, in the interests of his subject matter . . . and has to pay more and more attention to realities outside himself.

This stance immediately puts the pupil in a context and establishes that s/he has to step onto the starting block for education. If we are to confirm that this block can also be used for moral education, we have to look more closely at the processes involved here and ask whether they bear any relationship to what is necessary for moral education.

One way of doing this would be to look at the content of curricula: to analyse, for example, ways in which students are taught about national history (Does it admit past faults and oppression?) or biology (Is there an element of bioethics in the syllabus?) or whatever. Although it may be critically important that such opportunities for moral education and for cultivating moral competence be identified and maximised, they are yet peculiar to individual curricula and can themselves be handled in various ways. More importantly, in terms of Wilson's thesis, this approach fails to give the young person a methodology for addressing moral questions. It merely raises some of those questions. Thus we need to peel back further to examine what is essential for getting to grips with the curriculum.

The fundamental educational activity, I suggest, is that of confronting, assessing and reflecting on the evidence in whatever academic field, such as science or the arts, or mode, such as the hard intellectual or the emotional, this may be. Engaging in this activity depends upon certain virtues. For example, Telfer (1975) has articulated these as honesty, perseverance, carefulness and courage. Sockett (1988) identifies various "qualities of the will" (p. 196) which he regards as central, not only to the development of moral agency but also to education, which he defined as "the endeavor to get people to do things they could not previously do, to understand things they did not previously understand and, perhaps, to become people they did not expect to become" (p. 195). Sockett refers, *inter alia*, to the qualities of "endeavor, heed and control" (p. 199) which he argues are desirable *per se* as moral qualities and can be taught by schools. If schools are attending to the 'discipline' of learning (and here we remember that Wilson had much to say about various aspects of discipline, for example, see Wilson 1977), then they must, inevitably, model these virtues within the very pedagogical processes. (Here again we need to assume the difference between education and training as does Wilson, for example, see Wilson 1979). In order to pursue the truth of a subject, pupils must abandon their own prejudices, be open to others, be prepared to acknowledge that others have something to contribute, must care about 'getting things right' and not fudging the issues, and must recognise and take responsibility for mistakes.

Clearly, this point raises questions about the very pedagogic processes. Sockett argues that if the intellectual virtues are acquired inappropriately (he cites, for example Jackson's 1968 observation that young people can learn patience in school by waiting in lines, waiting for the bell, waiting for the teachers), then their general education will suffer just as much as their moral education. In this respect, the two are indistinguishable. The moral base of education is inherent in the structure of educational activity, rather then being an extension of it. In a later article, Sockett (1989) comments on the absence of "moral conversation and thought" in current educational language. Attempts to add something to the curriculum by way of moral education, or personal and social education, will fail if the addition is courted for its own sake rather than its dependence on the curriculum itself being acknowledged.

It is this particular aspect of connectedness that Wilson did not draw out explicitly, although he clearly acknowledged its desirability. This connectedness has the advantage that it can flourish in any context in which learning or education is taking place. It is attendant upon the educational activity itself, rather than upon particular social set-ups. This is not to deny that particular set-ups may be very potent, for example, the one that Wilson puts forward may bear similarities to the kibbutz or like community. But we are talking, essentially, about intensity. What we are not doing is excluding some people from the opportunity of experiencing the connectedness, which, arguably, is essential to a coherent moral education, just because they have no access to a particular social set-up such as the sort of school described by Wilson.

The possibility of this connectedness raises a host of questions which cannot adequately be dealt with here. For example, if they are serious about moral education, teachers will be serious about the integrity of their own teaching/educating: anything which is not strictly educational (and Wilson writes at length about the concept of education, see Wilson 1979) will not foster the intellectual virtues which transfer to equip the morally educated person. Senior managers, both internal and external to the institution, will consider this element in school evaluation. Interestingly, this is an aspect which Wilson does not address explicitly, but which is a logical consequence of much of what he proposes. Again, there are issues to do with initial teacher training (here, again, things have moved on a long way since Wilson (1975) wrote about it).

There are critical questions here as to whether teaching is about 'skills' or forwarding, perhaps presenting a commitment to, a *modus vivendi*. Much of the potency of the school Wilson delineated in *Practical Methods of Moral Education* was derived from the *community* element: the fact that teachers and students were living together and sharing time both inside and outside the classroom. Wilson sustains the theme of the potency of such relationships elsewhere (see Wilson, 1993). Such an arrangement affects the nature of the relationships, introducing or giving the opportunity for an element of honesty and trust, seeing others in a greater variety of emotional contexts, and a greater and richer range of dimensions. This is an advantage, I think, which is lacking in 'snapshot' worlds which focus on the readily measurable; certainly, it is exceedingly difficult to access. However, if Wilson is arguing that moral education within such a social set-up is available, then we need to ask, perhaps, whether such availability can be established within more conventional set-ups. Many have experienced such potent relationships but, again, I suggest their quintessence is implied in the very activity of teaching, rather than in any particular social arrangements or propitious meeting of minds which are sought for themselves or as a means to moral education ends.

Here we need to consider what goes on within the classroom or, more widely, within the school, in terms of 'educational care'. It seems to me that if we analyse this concept, we may have some vision of how *any* school, provided that it accepts certain necessary and logical points surrounding itself, *qua* school, can be fundamentally morally educative almost as a by-product of its 'ordinary' educational activity, as it were. It has been suggested that the virtues necessary for engaging in education resemble the components required for a morally educated person. The very process of educating actively engages participants in a moral activity and allows them to practise moral virtues. But in addition, there is, I would suggest, another way in which education is essentially moral. Again, much of what follows is explicit in Wilson's work but needs, perhaps, to be stated more overtly.

I may care passionately about my 'subject' but that, *per se*, need have no moral dimension. However, if I care not only for my subject but also that I enrich the lives of others by teaching them about it, educating them in it or whatever, then I am introducing a moral edge, provided, of course, that what I am teaching meets the general criteria of being educative, life-enhancing or 'worthwhile'. Throughout Wilson's writing, it is clear that he is dedicated to 'getting things right'. Those who know him personally, *qua* teacher, will recognize this trait. He engages in argument simply to get clear, not to win or show off his philosophical skills. However, what is not so clear in his writing is his dedication to being an educator. He is, perhaps, not entirely conscious of this because it is very much a part of him, *qua* person. Wilson is concerned that his own truth-seeking is shared with others. Indeed, at many times he would say that engagement with others is vital in order to 'get thing right'. Again, perhaps the interconnectedness, the moral edge, is inevitable rather than contingent. Perhaps we do not have to seek moral education in school, but, instead, merely recognise its manifestations. This sharing of truth is essentially moral, and is another reason why any school taking itself seriously as an educational institution will link the theoretical and practical approaches which Wilson sees as needing connecting and for which he suggested the model of the school, the viability of which in the present social context, we doubted earlier in this essay.

Were I, or Wilson, to be the sole possessor of the truth of the universe, namely, that the world is really run by little green men who manipulate humans as puppets, then however strong my belief in the truth and even the value of it to humans might be, there is surely no logical necessity for me to 'teach' others about the little green men and thus dispel their misapprehensions about what makes the world tick. I can go about in my own smug world, proud in my superior knowledge and indifferent or careless as to others' false beliefs. It is only when I so care that others get at the truth, and I acknowledge that they have an equal right to this, that I am moved to share my knowledge. This attitude, I would argue, is central to the concept of educator. The decision to teach, to help others develop the skills to get at the truth themselves rather than engage in the more isolated, albeit no less truth-seeking, business of research, again places the teacher on the starting block for moral education. It involves seeing the other as worthy of sharing the truth, of participating in a collaborative exercise, of handing over to others some of the power which sole possession of the truth represents, and thus inviting critical comment on one's own truth-pursuing activity and extending the opportunity to participate in the pursuit of truth. All this is grounded in concepts of justice, care and empowerment, some of the fundamentals of morally educating and developing the components of Wilson's morally educated person.

It is, of course, one thing to be at the starting position for education. Casual observation suggests, sadly, that many either do not realise the potential of the position or get distracted from the enterprise even if they start off with good intentions. In any case, the destination is obscure. It is a case, to use a tired cliche, where the value is in journeying rather than arriving. Conceptually, any point of arrival is uncertain. This is particularly the case with moral educating. This is implicit in Wilson's writing, stating as he does that the moral educator is in the business of equipping the student rather than aiming to mold a way of life or belief system. But again, this is what education does and what distinguishes it from training. Training may be a part of education, a means to an end, providing the necessary skills for engagement in the process, but only a part. Wilson's morally educated person is, in some ways, little different from his educated person in terms of broad approaches, although he emphatically maintained that the moral area was discrete, complementing, for example, the area of science or the humanities (see Wilson, 1993).

What is so immensely valuable and eternally relevant about Wilson's contributions to the philosophy of education is that underneath what may be to some a slightly intimidating style (intimidating in that it is uncompromising and demands attention, perhaps uncomfortably so, not allowing one to dither over his writing, but rather demanding reaction and response, not simply saying 'how interesting' before going and doing the shopping) are fundamentals which can be related to other scenarios or underpin the construction of other scenarios. He gives us little excuse to be 'roaring boys' for long.

References

Gardner, H. (1993) *Frames of Mind: The Theory of Multiple Intelligences.* London: Fontana Press.

Jackson, P. (1968) *Life In Classrooms.* New York: Holt, Rinehart and Winston.

Sockett, H. (1988) "Education and the Will: Aspects of Personal Capacity," *American Journal of Education,* 96, 2, 195 – 214.

Telfer, E. (1975) "Autonomy as an Educational Ideal," in Brown, S.C. (ed.), *Philosophers Discuss Education.* Totowa, N.J.: Rowman

Wilson, J. (1972a) *The Assessment of Morality.*
London: Heinemann
(1972b) *Practical Methods of Moral Education*
Windsor: NFER/Nelson.
(1975) *Educational Theory and the Preparation of Teachers*
Windsor: NFER/Nelson
(1977) *Philosophy and Practical Education*
London: Routledge, Kegan, Paul
(1979) *A Preface to the Philosophy of Education*
London; Routledge, Kegan, Paul
(1993) *Reflection and Practice*
London, Ontario: Althouse Press

Chapter Four

ℰℛ

The Public School Model

Henry Near

John Wilson's unending efforts to bridge the gaps often found between philosophy and educational practice deserve our appreciation and consideration. One way of bridging this gap is to show how education would be practised if derived from correct philosophical premises; in other words, to provide a model to be imitated or, at the least, aspired to. John Wilson has described such a model on several occasions:

> Schools as they could be . . . would have something of the potency . . . of the family, of certain schools in the independent sector. . . . Their crucial features [are] a strong house system or 'pastoral' base which overrides the classroom, a full-time investment on the part of the pupils, a deliberate shielding or separation of the institution from external practices and values. [RC&E, 12)

It needs scarcely be said that this model is based primarily on the English public school, an institution which John Wilson has known well as a schoolboy, as an undergraduate in an Oxford college largely peopled by former public-school pupils, and as a teacher. He has advocated this model at some length in two other books, suggesting that the public school should serve as a model for a vastly extended network of independent boarding schools, purged of the elements of privilege with which the present public schools are associated, and available to a wide selection of boys (he doesn't mention girls) chosen for their intellect and character. [PSPP, 42 - 108; PMME. pt. 4) In order not to confuse the model with the reality, let us call this Wilson's Ideal Public School or WIPS.

Over the years, in many private conversations with me, John Wilson has expressed his interest in a similar system of education, that of the kibbutz movement; and, although he has scarcely referred to it in his writings, his use of the term 'communal education' for the public school system hints at the belief that these are two variants of a similar educational approach. I think that I must be in an almost unique position to assess this comparison because I was educated at a minor public school, spent four years at Oxford in close contact with John and his fellow Wykehamists, and have spent much of the rest of my life teaching, researching and bringing up my children within the kibbutz educational system. I should, therefore, like to offer some reflections about the idea and practice of communal education, in its British and Israeli forms. Like John Wilson, I shall deal mainly with the secondary level, ages 13 - 18, though there is also much to say about the younger ages.

In the classic period of kibbutz education, roughly from the mid-1920s until the mid-1960s, there were three separate kibbutz movements, each with its own educational system. That of the Kibbutz Artzi was the most similar to the British public school: the children, boys and girls, lived in boarding schools, within a radius of some twenty miles of their home kibbutzim, visiting their parents two or three times a week. In addition to their formal schooling, they took part in a wide variety of extra-curricular activities, all based on the 'educational institute', as the boarding schools were called. Though games played little part in the life of the school, there was an equivalent activity in work: the pupils worked either on the educational farm in the school area or in their home kibbutzim on one day during the six-day working week for a number of hours suited to their age.

This system was based on a well-defined educational model. Its initiators had been members and leaders of a Zionist youth movement, through which they had found their way to Israel and the kibbutz. They believed that, in the period of adolescence, young people are uniquely able to create for themselves a system of social values free from the conformism, contradictions and hypocrisies of adult society. They themselves had done this in their youth movement life, and they believed that their children should be educated in a framework as much like the youth movement as possible. Thus, for instance, the geographical distance from their home kibbutzim would enable the youngsters to build for themselves their own concept of an ideal society, free from the blemishes of the real kibbutz. There was a developed system of curricular studies, taught to a great extent by progressive methods, but the activities of the 'young people's society' were considered crucial to the development of a social ethic which would fit the pupils for their future life in the kibbutz.

This theoretical model of an independent and democratic society of adolescents did not accord entirely with school practice. From the first, the teachers and house-mothers played an important role, as did leaders and adult advisers in the youth movement on which the educational institute was modeled. Nor did the physical separation from the home kibbutz necessarily lead to independent development. Contact with parents and the real kibbutz was always of great importance, and provided role models that did not always accord with the ideas of the educational authorities. But, on the whole, the system worked well, and produced a generation of young people imbued with kibbutz principles and ready to function as a serving elite in Israeli society, as had their parents before them.

Neither of the other two movements accepted the principle of the independence of youth or built boarding schools on the model of the Kibbutz Artzi. But their educational set-up was similar in several respects: in almost all kibbutzim, the children slept away from their parents in quarters specially built for children or young people, under the care of a *metapelet,* the kibbutz equivalent of a house-mother; and the youth movement idea, with its typical structure of small educational groups and, in older age, the 'young people's society', was the basis for a wide-ranging programme of extra-curricular activities.

Thus, in many respects the kibbutz system was similar to that of the public school, though there were many differences, particularly in content and in teaching methods, which were specially marked in the more formal aspects of educational theory and practice. John Wilson was quite right when he hinted that there is a common basis to these two systems: both of them are structured in such a way as to ensure a great deal of interaction and joint activity on the part of the children, and these activities create a common ethos and a complex of social values which are a vital part of the school's tradition.

There are, however, important differences in the way in which communal education is advocated and defended. Wilson enumerates seven reasons for anchoring moral education in the school community [PMME, 105]. Most of them are concerned directly with the relationship between the pupils: their need for a secure framework in terms of group-identity and for a personal identity; the need to channel and institutionalise aggression, and the importance of cooperation, and of pupils' participation, presumably in group activities. The other defined needs are for parent-figures, close contact with adults, and a firmly defined authority. But the thrust of the argument is the importance of strong inter-personal relationships and activities among the pupils. It is strengthened by reference to the many manifestations of such relationships among teenagers, even though they are demoted to the status of "symptoms of our failure" to fulfill their needs, rather than positive phenomena in their own right. [PMME, 107].

The Israeli experience, and the theory which accompanies it, is similarly derived from the existence and positive effects of inter-personal and group relationships at the stage of adolescence [Near, YM&KE]. But it places a much greater emphasis on such relationships. Historically, the Zionist youth movements aspired to function, not as a supplement or even a corrective to the conventional educational system, but as a substitute for it. They believed that, at this stage of their life, young people could and should create for themselves a value-system which would shape the course of their future lives. Indeed, this is exactly what happened to the founders of the kibbutz movement and the youth movements which provided their manpower reserves.

In fact, neither the 'youth communities' nor the pioneering youth movements were as autonomous as this theory postulated. In the youth movement, leaders at all levels influenced their young charges deeply, and imposed their ideology on the movement as a whole. In the kibbutz high schools, including the relatively isolated boarding schools, the educators and *metaplot* (in public school language, house-masters and house-mothers) played a similar role; perhaps even more so than in the public schools, since the educators were usually also teachers. A conscious attempt was made to integrate social studies in the formal curriculum with the ideas and ideals propounded in the extra-curricular activities modeled on the youth movement.

In contrast to this, John Wilson derives the theory of WIPS from another model, not the youth movement, but the family [PMME, 104 – 111]. There would seem to be a basic contradiction in this contention, that is, that children are torn from the bosom of the family, with all the emotional suffering and psychological consequences involved in this process, in order to spend his or her most impressionable and, in many respects, the most vulnerable years within a simulated family! The arguments advanced in favour of this operation seem very weak: parents don't devote enough time to their children, many families break up, and children don't see their parents at work. These would surely be reasons for perfecting a model of WIF or Wilson's Ideal Family and considering how it could be achieved in practice, perhaps in ways like those currently advocated by the Communitarian movement, rather than removing the children altogether from the family environment.

In terms of theory, the kibbutz model is more consistent. In the youth movement, the nuclear or 'bourgeois' family was seen as oppressive, egoistic, hypocritical and culturally philistine. It was, therefore, necessary to limit its influence and isolate the younger generation from it as much as possible. In the kibbutz, many, particularly educators influenced by Freudian theory, believed that there was a conflict between the nuclear family and communal society and between the needs of the child and the 'pathogenic' relationships within the family. Although this opposition was toned down over the years, the place of the family within the kibbutz has always been a matter of controversy. And the kibbutz boarding school aimed to minimise not only the influence of the real kibbutz as against the ideal society evolved by the pupils and their educators, but also that of the nuclear family, which could well, and not infrequently did, deviate from the norms of the collective. These are surely far more cogent arguments for boarding schools, of whatever sort, that those which John Wilson puts forward.

In fact, the nuclear family proved to be stronger than the theory. Even in the most extreme movement, the Kibbutz Artzi, children spent several hours every day with their parents until the age of thirteen, and visited their home kibbutzim several times each week during the boarding school period. In the less extreme kibbutz movements, anti-familiar arguments were rarely used. But in all the movements, the influence of the children's community and of movement-type activities was considered to be a major, indeed, *the* major factor, in moral and social education.

We have, therefore, three different theoretical arguments for communal education. In the Wilsonian version, communal education builds upon an amended form of the family; in the extreme kibbutz version, it serves as a substitute for the family; and, in the real kibbutz, it acts as an independent framework co-existing with the family.

There is enough empirical evidence to show that, in any of these forms, communal education does, or could do, the job which John Wilson assigns it, that is, the formation of a shared code of ethics. That Wilson's model, WIPS, can accomplish this aim follows, *a fortiori*, from the evidence of the real public schools. That the kibbutz models, whatever the philosophical views of their educators, can do the same shows forth in the character and accomplishments of successive generations of kibbutz-born youngsters. [Near, SD] These types of evidence point to the importance of the nature of the activities and interaction between pupils which takes place in the communal framework.

One of the principal, and most characteristic, features of youth movement education is the small, educational group or, in Scouting parlance, the patrol. Here young people learn the social skills required for life in a close-knit community, and experience in its most intensive form the 'inner exhilaration' which is one of the typical attributes of the classic youth movement. This is the basis of the 'communal experience', the feeling of strong comradeship, which is a vital ingredient of kibbutz life. It is

> A semi-mystical experience arising spontaneously from the actions and interactions of people—particularly young people—in small groups. It can be the result of working together, of singing or dancing together, of the sort of discussion in which "soul touches soul." History also shows us that it can be the result of fighting together in the form of **esprit de corps**. The great majority of those who undergo it feel it to be positive, significant, and worthy of repeating if possible. [Near, CE]

In the literature of the kibbutz and the pioneering youth movements, this experience is given many names, among them, 'love', 'eros', 'the communal act', and various versions of 'together'. Following Schmalenbach, one of the few scholars who has dealt with this experience in any depth, I shall call it 'communion'. [OC] It is a major key to understanding why people live in kibbutzim and other communal societies.

Such experiences were a prime factor in the educational practice both of the youth movements which fed the kibbutzim and of the kibbutz educational system. They take place most typically during youth. But they have far-reaching influence on the overall quality of kibbutz life, creating deep emotional bonds between the members. These bonds are seen particularly clearly at times of common rejoicing, such as festivals and weddings, and of common sorrow, such as illness and death. They form the substratum of mutual relationships in almost every field of life, from communal economic enterprises to the virtually complete social security which characterizes the kibbutz community and, in fact, all communal societies. Though the strength and frequency of such experiences tend to wane with age, it is hard to envisage a viable commune without the element of communion.

Communion is the core experience of the youth movement and, in various degrees of intensity, of all forms of collective education. In the classic pioneering youth movement, it is linked to the ideology of juventism: the belief that the ideas and experiences of youth are uniquely valid and should be incorporated into a radically new adult society. This motivation led to the development of the kibbutz movement [Near, YM&KE]. In other educational frameworks, including the public schools, the Boy Scouts and other youth organizations, this motivation is harnessed to 'education for leadership' in which a stress on the values of cooperation, mutual help and mutual regard is seen to be entailed, psychologically, if not necessarily logically, by the experience of communion. It should be stressed at this point that the adult leaders, supervisors and educators play a vital role in the translation of these values into more concrete terms: Zionism and the kibbutz, in the case of the pioneering youth movement; special ideological and social doctrines, in the case of other youth movements; and the British upper-class ethos, in the case of the public schools.

What are the results of this process? In observing graduates of the kibbutz system and of several public schools, I have been impressed by the many similarities among them. I am not alone in this. One of the few people who has had similar opportunities for such comparison was Dorothea Krook, a Cambridge don who married one of the first graduates of the school in kibbutz Ein Harod, and who lived in that kibbutz for the rest of her life. Claiming that the kibbutz-born were the aristocrats of Israel, she described them as

> Intelligent, but not distinctly intellectual . . . [not stupid-looking, as some claim, since] the 'stupid' look is the product of tranquillity, the composure, the absence of anxiety which springs from their absolute, never-questioned security in their material surroundings. . . . They have never been anything but active, busy, fully employed: first in play and study . . . then Army service, then back to their life's work on the estate or in public life or both.

Replying to the widespread charge that the kibbutz-born are a 'snobbish in-group, taking credit for the achievements of their parents and grandparents', Krook maintains that these very characteristics show them to be a true aristocracy.

> Their virtue is, or is becoming, 'hereditary' . . . it positively demands the active, personal, individual re-creation of the heritage [derived from the founders of the kibbutzim]. . . . It is not directed exclusively to the moral and spiritual guidance of the community, but loves to exercise itself also in the active, practical spheres of government and national defence. [RT, 337 – 9]

Of course, this is an idealized picture, both of kibbutz youth and of 'historic aristocracies' at their supposed best, but it is sufficiently close to the truth to be recognizable. Let us call this model, KIA or Krook's Ideal Aristocracy.

In the context of this essay, the significant element is not the parallel between the social background of the two sets of people, but the fact that, in both cases, they are the product of communal education. Young men and women are drawn from a very different background, (for instance, the Youth Aliya scheme, in whose framework children from under-privileged families are educated in the kibbutz) *acquiring* the ways of thoughts and behaviour of the kibbutz-born in the course of their four or six years of communal education. It is easy to distinguish between the kibbutz-born and others of similar age who joined the kibbutz in adulthood. In all of these cases the social background, including all the elements which Krook adduces as characteristic of the aristocracy, is the same. However, it is only those educated in the kibbutz framework who think, feel and act like Krook's aristocrats.

In both the British and the Israeli case, the behaviour and thought-patterns of the graduates of the communal educational system are those of a privileged minority, but a minority which is brought up to believe that its privileges must be paid for by giving the appropriate service to the state, whether in the Army, the Civil Service or Colonial Service in the case of the KIA, or military service in special units, new settlements or other public activities with the kibbutz-born.

In the accustomed jargon, one usually refers to the kibbutz, including its younger generation, as a serving elite within Israeli society. There is no doubt that, in return, the kibbutz has received many privileges over the years. But there is much truth in Krook's assertion that the kibbutz is, in fact if not in theory, a hereditary elite, closer to the pattern of the aristocracy than, for instance, a meritocratic class or even one which wins its social predominance by economic success. Although, in principle, the kibbutz-born are not automatically admitted to membership, in fact, virtually all of those who choose to join the kibbutz as adults are accepted as members by the general assembly or in a ballot of all the members. They owe their social status and their share in the economic assets of the kibbutz to birth rather than to any criterion of intelligence or achievement.

In the context of the educational questions we are considering here, the way the minority is chosen is of less importance than the fact that it *is* a minority. This point would not, of course, apply to WIPS, though it is an essential part of KIA. The question arises whether it is possible, in fact or in principle, to apply the methods of communal education to a very much wider population, perhaps, in fact, to the whole of a given age-group. The concept of WIPS assumes that it is. In my view, the experience of the pioneering youth movements and the kibbutz show that it is not.

There were two salient facts about the pioneering youth movements in the classic period. Young people joined them, and then left them. If one estimates their power and educational influence in terms of the number of young Jews aged thirteen and over who passed through their ranks in the twenties and thirties, the numbers were very great, perhaps as many as a third of those in the relevant age-groups in the countries of Eastern Europe. But if the criterion is the number who actually did what their movements demanded of them and joined kibbutzim, the figures are very much smaller, no more than one in eight or ten. Of these, many left the kibbutz shortly after their arrival in Palestine. Part of the explanation lies in the fact that they were called to live a life of physical hardship. But it was more than that. Here, too, Dorothea Krook discerned an essential point. She quotes a kibbutz-born woman as saying,

I had thirty years of it, and I couldn't stand any more. . . . I got sick of having my personal affairs, and other people's personal affairs, discussed, weighed, and considered by everybody. It just became too much for me, the endless communality, the constant exposure, the lack of privacy.

Krook comments,

It is heartening to think that there are at least 90,000 people in the world who do not find it oppressive, or at least endurable, or at worst a blessed yoke. But that it is a yoke few people of the kibbutzim will deny, nor that it is perhaps the most rigorous sacrifice the kibbutz society exacts—and, of course, necessarily exacts—from its members, compared with which living in a shack or doing without a refrigerator is a minor deprivation indeed. It is also no doubt the final reason that the majority of freedom-loving, choice-exercising men and women will never consent to join a society which they may—for other people—. . . exalt and admire. [RT, 330]

The crucial words in this acute observation are "necessarily exacts": the lack of privacy, the intense communal interaction within the educational group, the kibbutz school, and (less intensely in day-to-day life but, in the long run, no less irksomely for many) in kibbutz life, is the unavoidable concomitant of the experience of communion. Just as there are those for whom communion is key to a new life, so are there many who experience it and reject it absolutely. This is one of the major reasons why both the youth movements and the kibbutzim lost members from their very beginnings: selectivity or, more exactly, self-selection, was inherent in their very being.

Therefore, the youth movement model failed as a framework for the education of a whole generation of the kibbutz-born. The founders of the kibbutzim expected their children to create for themselves a world-outlook and set of values similar to those which they themselves had created in the youth movement. But, like the youth movement, the educational system demanded that these young people, all of them, accept the 'blessed yoke' of communion and the way of life it entails. For a variety of historical reasons, until the mid-seventies, more than fifty per cent of kibbutz-born men and women returned to the kibbutzim after their army service. Since then, the numbers have been declining, and show no signs of rising again. Clearly, many have rejected communalism, despite the fact that they were educated in a framework designed to promote and perpetuate it.

For, attractive though communion is to many, there is no knowing in advance which child will be attracted by communion and which repelled, just as there is no knowing in advance which adults will persevere in communal living. In this sense, universal communal education bears the seeds of its own, at least partial, destruction.

For this reason, WIPS cannot be a model for a widely extended educational system. It could, however, serve as a method of selection for an elite, chosen on grounds not of wealth, birth or other forms of social privilege, but of readiness to live according to communal virtues such as mutual aid or a desire to serve the outside community. Such an elite would have to be, at least in part, self-selected, as was the elite which was crystallized in the youth movements and led the kibbutz movement for many years. In this process, educators, house-mothers and others, including the family, would play a part. But the primary decision, for or against communion as a central ingredient in their life, must be made by the pupils themselves. They must be free to stay in the system or leave it, with full awareness of the implications of their choice.

Whether such a system is possible in Great Britain, I cannot say. It could be achieved in the kibbutz movement, if communal education were not to be the immutable rule as it is, with very few exceptions, at present. Near's Ideal Kibbutz Education (NIKE) would be based on the youth movement as it was in its prime. Pupils would be given the opportunity of staying within the system or leaving it, and given feasible alternatives if they left. Those who remained would form an elite within the kibbutz movement, no doubt a much smaller one than it is today, to be augmented by others recruited from the youth movements and other sources.

The use of such a model also raises the question of the family. In my view, the experience of the kibbutz movement has proved that there is not an inevitable contradiction between communal education and the institution of the family. If the system is properly conducted, pupils can live in communal dormitories or boarding-schools during adolescence while visiting their families daily. This routine still leaves plenty of time for the essential institutions of the children's society to function, and the conflicts between the family and community can fit well into the process of preparation for life as it really is.

Finally, I shall add a short comment on one aspect of WIPS which has an important bearing on the function of the school in society. John Wilson clearly sees this school, especially the independent school, as an instrument for changing society. He sees in WIPs, perhaps even in the existing public schools,

> a deliberate shielding or separation of the institution from external practices and values . . . **in the teeth of** external pressures whether of ideological intervention or the values of the market-place. [RC&E,12]

Such a view is surely at variance with the nature of the existing school system or of any that might replace it. In the case of the public school, to say that the institution as such is shielded or separated from external systems and values seems to me to be very far from the truth about this or any other method of schooling. It is true that, in matters of curriculum, teaching methods and the like, the school may set its own standards and priorities. For example, the teaching of Greek and Latin, though it has been part of the public school tradition for centuries, may be abandoned and replaced by biology and computer science. But this change will not affect the communal structure of the school which is the key to its special function, as John Wilson rightly says.

Neither in the intentions of the great majority of educators nor in the consciousness and attitudes of those pupils with whom the system has been most successful is it possible to distinguish clearly between the effectiveness of the system as such and the values it intends to promote and very largely succeeds in promoting. Esprit de corps, patriotism, a willingness to take on public service, all of these are the characteristics of the ideal 'public school man'. In Wilson's own account as in the accepted image and self-image, these are the end results of the prefectoral system, the emphasis on games, and the intimacy of communal living. These qualities and attitudes are, essentially, the mark of an elite, the one which, historically, was at the head of the administration and armed forces of Britain and the British Empire and, currently, remains at the core of the British social elite, the business/political middle and upper class. True, in intellectual matters the public school boy is encouraged to develop an independent mind which has led many of them, including John Wilson himself, to question these notions, and in many cases, even to rebel against them. But the results of public school education are overwhelmingly to produce conformist, upper-class citizens. This, in itself, is in line with Wilson's own views when he emphasizes the vital function of the school's structure in promoting moral and, in this context, political values.

None of this is news. The social function of any school must be, in general, to promote the values and ideals of the society which affords it legal and social legitimation, and, no less, its financial backing. Such values could be different, as Wilson suggests, in a situation where public-type schools were used to promote democratic and egalitarian values. But this difference would be a result, not of independent actions and policies on the part of teachers and pupils in the WIPS, but of political decisions. Similarly, the educational establishment in the kibbutz movements enjoyed a good deal of leeway in deciding on curriculum, on the structure of the school, and on such matters as the degree in which kibbutz education conformed to the demands of the state educational authorities; for instance, whether to prepare the pupils for the matriculation examination. Economic and social pressure to adapt the system to contemporary developments in kibbutz society have wrought changes which some have described as the abandonment of the unique character of kibbutz education. It could not have been otherwise. For, in the long run, no society will pay, in money, manpower or prestige, for institutions which tend, as even in the case of WIPS, or aspire to undermine its foundation.

In this essay, I have not discussed the problems of the real kibbutz, or the developments now taking place in a kibbutz society and communal education. All I have tried to show is that, though its theoretical underpinnings require modification, WIPS could be a reasonable model for high school education. But, as every sneakered schoolboy knows, NIKE is better.

References

CD   H. Near, "The Collective Experience: Universal and Particular," in D. Hardy and L. Davidson (eds.), *Utopian Thought and Communal Experience*, Middlesex Polytechnic Geography and Planning Paper, No. 24, 1989, 37 – 43

OC   H. Schmalenbach, "On Communion," in G. Luschen and G.P. Stone, *Schmalenbach on Society and Experience*, Chicago, 1977.

PMME   J. Wilson, *Practical Methods of Moral Education*, London, 1972.

PS&PP   J. Wilson, *Public Schools and Private Practice*, London, 1962.

RC&E   J. Wilson, "Race, Culture and Education: Some Conceptual Problems," *Oxford Review of Education*, 12, 1 (1986), 3 – 15.

RT   D. Krook, "Rationalism Triumphant: An Essay on the Kibbutzim of Israel," in P. King and B.C. Parekh (eds.), *Politics and Experience*, Cambridge, 1986, 309 – 41.

SD   H. Near, *The Seventh Day*, London, 1968.

YM&KE   H. Near, "Youth Movements and Kibbutz Education," in F.M. Konard, L. Liegle and Y. Dror (eds.), *Erziehungsreform in Deütschland und Israel*, Tubingen, forthcoming.

Educational Research

Chapter Five

Being a Bit Pregnant: How Philosophical Misconceptions Lead to Stillborn Empirical Research

Robin Barrow

I. Prophylactics

I have admired John Wilson, a very human philosopher, and his work ever since I first read his *Equality* (1966) as an undergraduate. He has never wavered from his commitment to philosophical analysis and his writing is always lucid, free of jargon, and, above all, interesting. It is interesting mainly because of the wide range of his concerns and his ability to draw on this breadth of understanding, and to write as a sophisticated, but commonsensical, man of intelligence would talk. There are points on which Wilson and I have disagreed, and others on which we still do. (There will be an instance of each below). But our differences are *within* the discipline of philosophy.

In regard to points of agreement, we take a very similar view of the nature and significance of the discipline itself, and we share essentially the same conception of education (see, e.g., Wilson, 1979 and 1986; Barrow, 1981 and 1984). We are also at one in believing that it is no accident that, therefore, we have essentially similar views on empirical educational research (see, e.g. Wilson 1972, 1975 and 1993; Barrow, 1976, 1984 and 1990). Specifically, we maintain that philosophic sophistication is a logically necessary condition for any worthwhile educational research. First, because some leading research questions are philosophical, rather than empirical (which is why, throughout this paper, I often have to use the cumbersome phrase, "empirical educational research," rather than simply, "research"); secondly, because, generally speaking, the more complex and interesting empirical questions cannot be adequately dealt with in the absence of competent philosophical groundwork. We also hold that, contingently, such competence is all too often lacking.

Four preliminary points need to be made in light of those remarks. First, I am not endorsing the naive and untenable belief that some issues are purely empirical and others purely philosophical and non-empirical. An 'empirical' issue, by which I mean for present purposes no more than an issue that can be examined or determined by some form of experiment and/or observation, is never, strictly speaking, *purely* or *simply,* empirical. Indeed, it one of the basic points of my argument that there are always conceptual questions that are logically integral to assessing the coherence of empirical claims. Even the claim that a person died as a result of a gunshot wound to the heart, depends for its truth partly on such things as what constitutes death, and that is not a purely empirical issue, although in the past we have been accustomed to thinking of it as such. That assumption, that it is a purely empirical question, was the product of widespread agreement on criteria in a relatively stable and straightforward world. But increased empirical understanding of such things as the different role that the brain stem and the cerebellum play, and increased ability to do such things as keep brain-dead people 'alive' for giving birth, for example, dramatically open up the question of what is to count as 'being dead' (Singer, 1994). While answering that question demands knowledge of various empirical points, it is ultimately a matter of judgement or decision in the light of these facts. It is a conceptual matter. Conversely, as the example also illustrates, a conceptual matter is not totally divorced from empirical considerations: our concept of 'death' must take account of what is the case empirically. For example, what does happen when only a person's brain stem is still intact? My distinction, therefore, between the empirical and the conceptual is not an absolute one. However, it remains reasonable, and, as I shall be arguing, crucial to recognize the difference between the two. For practical purposes in many cases we can reasonably classify a problem as being essentially empirical *or* conceptual, depending upon whether the conceptual or the empirical aspects are deemed relatively uncontentious. Thus (and, incidentally, to make such distinctions as this is itself partly a matter of judgement), the question of whether the gunshot wound was the cause of death may generally be classified as empirical, because, generally, notwithstanding what I have said above, there is no dispute that the victim is what we would call 'dead'. Conversely, the question of whether a person is well-educated is likely to be primarily a conceptual question, because for the most part we are arguing, not about what has happened to the individual during their upbringing or what they can do, but what is to count as 'being educated'.

Secondly, by way of preliminaries, it should be noted that the phrase, "an empirical question," is ambiguous. We may refer to something as an empirical question, meaning that it is a question to be answered, if it can be, by means of experiment and observation, or we may mean that it is a question of fact as opposed to judgement or opinion. The latter sense, though it is quite common, is problematic in various ways, and I shall not use the phrase, "an empirical question," in this way. When I refer to "an empirical question," I mean a question that, insofar as we hope to answer it, will require primarily some process of experiment and/or observation.

Thirdly, it should also be recognised that empirical research can itself make a contribution to conceptual refinement. But it should be apparent that the extent to which empirical findings can contribute to conceptual understanding is dependant on the extent to which a given field or area of inquiry is otherwise conceptually clear and secure. Thus, though one does not dispute that scientific theory and concepts are by no means entirely uncontentious (Phillips, 1987), in broad terms the physical sciences, being relatively developed disciplines, can quite often increase understanding of a concept through empirical discovery. If, for example, we have a clear and uncontentious concept of a certain species of animal, then empirical research may reveal a further feature that is common to all members of the species. The further step of regarding this feature as a defining characteristic of the species is still a matter of judgement or decision, but one would not dispute that the empirical discovery may be what gives rise to any such change in our conception. However, the social sciences and various other areas of human inquiry are often in a far less secure position in this respect (see Phillips, 1976; Searle, 1995). For example, if we were to discover that all happy people have a great deal of self-confidence, then we might be led to consider defining happiness partly in terms of that self-confidence, just as if we discovered that all horses had some hitherto undetected physical feature, we could consider making that feature a criterion of what constitutes a horse. But, whereas, in the latter case there is not much dispute about the current understanding of what a horse is and, let us assume, not much dispute about the nature of the newly discovered criterion, in the former case there is considerable dispute and uncertainty as to what constitutes 'happiness' and 'self-confidence'. Consequently, the alleged empirical discovery is itself highly questionable, since the question, "Do happy people have self-confidence?" is, with the qualifications I have referred to, not primarily an empirical question, but a conceptual one (Barrow, 1980).

My final preliminary point is that, though certain specific questions raised in the field of education may be empirical, the field of study as a whole obviously cannot be accounted a form of natural science, and most of its key questions are not empirical (that is, dependant for resolution on experiment and/or observation without much significant need for conceptual work). What 'education' is, what the field is, is not an empirical question, as we have seen. Since educational concerns are also intimately bound up with ethical and evaluative judgments in respect of human interactions, as opposed to mere behaviours, it is evident that research in the area must begin with a great deal of philosophical groundwork.

Let these preliminaries serve as prophylactics against subsequent confusion and error.

II. Quantitative Research

Wilson's argument is that much empirical educational research is vitiated by the fact that the basic conceptual work is either not done or done very inadequately. If it were done properly, we would see that, in many cases, the mode of investigation chosen is inappropriate, and, in some cases, we would see that no form of empirical investigation could be appropriate (see Wilson 1968, 1971, 1975, 1979, 1986, and 1993). If, for example, we wish to investigate a question such as whether teenagers are more prone to falling in love in one society than another, it is surely self-evident that we cannot proceed without some account of what constitutes 'being in love'.[1] If we were to determine that 'being in love' is to be defined in terms of such characteristics as being sexually excited by the thought or presence of the loved one, daydreaming, experiencing pangs of jealousy, and passing sleepless nights, then any empirical inquiry worth taking seriously must be an inquiry into these matters. Furthermore, the defining characteristics that are being investigated must themselves be conceptually clear. We cannot observe, monitor, measure or otherwise empirically research sexual excitement without a clear idea of what counts as sexual excitement. The specific mode(s) of investigation employed, the particular instruments used, must be appropriate to the object of inquiry. In some cases, it should be apparent that the object in question is not, in fact, amenable to any direct observation or to any empirical procedure. One might suggest, for instance, that whether a person is jealous cannot be directly observed. If, in order to proceed empirically, we draw up a list of behavioural indicators of jealousy, then it is clear that the quality of our research is primarily dependent on the plausibility of our conceptions of jealousy and the argument we produce to link these indicators with the concept.

Many an old joke revolves around the idea of being a bit pregnant. Can one be a bit pregnant? No, of course not, because pregnancy is defined as a state of being that either obtains or it does not. The same is true of death. We should not be confused by the point already mentioned that there may be dispute as to what constitutes death or pregnancy, and therefore borderline cases when we are not sure what to say. Whatever constitutes death or pregnancy, they just are terms that refer to a state that does not allow of degree. There are many terms of which this is not so, degree-words such as happiness and love which, it may be argued, are, by definition, not all or nothing affairs: in principle, one can be more or less happy, but not more or less pregnant.[2]

In a recent television program, an exchange took place that is symptomatic of the widespread confusion on the basic point made in the previous paragraph.[3] An interviewer asked a university professor who specialised in the study of psychopaths whether one could be "a bit psychopathic." "That's an empirical question," came the crisp reply, to which we don't yet have the answer. But, of course, it is not an empirical question, that is, one that we are now ready to investigate empirically. As the professor had himself just said, "there are many different definitions of a psychopath." So long as we do not have an agreed definition, the empirical aspect of the question cannot be meaningfully pursued. If we did have an agreed definition, it is possible that it would be a definition of an absolute state, comparable, in this respect, to death and pregnancy. In this case, empirical inquiry would be logically irrelevant.

In the absence of an agreed definition, individual researchers, such as the professor in question, provide their own. But often, as in this case, they do not engage properly in the philosophical task of reasoning towards a conception. Rather they produce an instrument, a check list, of characteristics that they associate with the psychopath. That instrument or check list thus defines the object of inquiry. Any such approach is liable to be open to further objections, for example, that characteristics of the type, 'lacks empathy' or 'rejects value systems other than his own', are themselves conceptually unclear and not directly ascertainable by empirical means. If, in response to that criticism, the concepts are rendered clear and observable by defining them in terms of unambiguous behavioural indicators, we see the same problems arising at one remove.

In an attempt to define 'psychopath', the creating of such an instrument might be very useful, provided that the philosophical argument for the creation of the instrument remains the focus of our attention. In practice, however, the argument for the nature of a particular instrument in such research is seldom, if ever, provided. If it is, the argument is barely recognisable as a philosophical one. As an attempt to help us locate psychopaths, the instrument is necessarily useless; though it is conceivable that it might be a useful instrument. In respect of defining the terms, the question of whether it is entirely philosophical depends upon whether this is what we believe we should define as a 'psychopath'.

Small wonder, then, that an individual, judged by the instrument in question to be a psychopath and interviewed in the same programme, seemed somewhat frustrated. It was not in doubt that he and some friends had robbed a store and then drugged themselves to the eyeballs; nor that when they saw one of their number clearly dying of an overdose, they left him to die rather than call the police. But does that make the man a psychopath? He thought not, because, in general, he thought that he had empathy. In addition, the individual thought that some, but not all, of society's rules, were worth keeping. I, of course, cannot possibly pass judgement on whether he was a psychopath. But I can make the obvious and vitally important point that he has been stereotyped with a label that will have very far-reaching conclusions for no very good reason.

The charge against much empirical research in education is that, in the absence of any adequate analysis of key concepts such as 'education', 'an effective school', 'a traditional/progressive mode of teaching', 'learning how to learn', 'critical thinking', 'intelligence' and 'good teaching', the methodology of research in practice defines the concepts. Intelligence, to focus on a familiar example, is defined by intelligence tests. The tail wags the dog. Not only should a concept such as intelligence not be defined by the instruments used to measure it, but it may be the case that proper reflection on the concept will lead us to see that, in important respects, it is not something that can be measured in any systematic way at all. Intelligence, as I have argued elsewhere, can indeed by *judged*, but it is a matter of estimating, interpreting, understanding and so forth, rather than a straightforward observation or measurement (Barrow, 1993).

Such a claim does not involve a denial of the palpable fact that one's intelligence—whatever precisely we take the word to mean—is dependant on a host of physical and neurophysiological factors, and that empirical inquiry is necessary for a fuller understanding of the phenomenon. How we precisely define the term, however, is ultimately a matter of philosophical reasoning and decision making, involving amongst other things certain value judgements. In this respect, an intelligence test is comparable to a urine test for pregnancy, with the difference that 'pregnancy' is a less contentious concept so that we may be more confident of the empirical research establishing a urine test as a reasonably reliable, indirect test for it. In the case of 'intelligence', there is no such agreement on the concept. The philosophical work that has been done on the concept is ignored by empirical researchers. Whatever reasoning they have to support claims, either that the items on their test are indirect indicators or that those items define the concept, is not provided.

The consequences of this failure to recognise that the key concepts in the educational enterprise are complex, contentious and require proper philosophical analysis before one can proceed to empirical investigation relating to them, include a variety of confusions and errors. Sometimes investigators present a logical claim as an empirical one. Sometimes they inadequately define a concept in behavioural terms. What results is a domain of empirical research in education which provides conclusions that, at best, cannot be agreed to be founded on a reasonable conception of what it is to be educated and, at worst, are founded on a concept of something other than education. Similarly, the all-important question of whether more specific research is indeed research into what it purports to be remains entirely unresolved. (Barrow, 1984).

III. Philosophical Analysis

Commitment to this view of educational empirical research and its *de facto* shortcomings raises the question of the nature of philosophical analysis. I have referred repeatedly to the need for "proper" or "adequate" analysis. Since nobody disputes that empirical researchers define their terms, either explicitly or implicitly in their choice of instruments, one must ask: What is proper analysis?

Wilson has been criticised for seeming to take the position that, while good analysis of complex concepts is undoubtedly a difficult business, it is unproblematic in the sense that if you do the job properly, your analysis of 'education', for example, will reveal what education necessarily and truly *is*. To his critics, this position is a terrible, even a facile, mistake. There is, they would say, no *true* account of what education is: there are merely competing conceptions, the product of differing time, place and individual perspective. The so-called sociology of knowledge (it should have been called the sociology of belief), drawing incidentally on a line of reasoning that dates back to Heraclitus and Thrasymachus in Plato's *Republic*, but coming to the fore in the late sixties, popularised the basic Marxist contention that our concepts are ultimately the product of economic and power structures in society. Postmodernism offers a much more variegated, even anarchic, picture of the diverse factors that may lead different individuals to hold the conceptions that they do. But, whatever the precise theory about the sources of our conceptions, the essential criticism remains the same: education is not what it is in some absolute and transcendental sense, but whatever some culture, society or individual believes it to be. If that is so, it may be argued, the empirical researcher cannot be open to the criticism that he has failed to analyse the concept properly, provided it is clear what he takes the term in question to mean.

One of the points about which Wilson and I disagree is whether it makes sense to say that a given conception is true, whether, for example, one can talk about the true meaning of 'education' (see Barrow 1983, 1985; Wilson 1985). I believe that the notion of a true conception is meaningless, and consequently that what I refer to as proper or adequate analysis is not to be understood in terms of arriving at the correct conception. But, while Wilson still seems to want to argue that such terms do make sense, the extent to which he and I agree in relation to the issue of philosophical analysis is far more important than the extent to which we disagree, and is quite sufficient to explain the nature of the failure of empirical researchers to do the job properly.

Neither Wilson nor I, incidentally, dispute the truth of the sociological claim that, as a matter of fact, different circumstances may lead to different beliefs. Neither of us deny, more particularly, that different cultures have had or do have differing views of education. But we argue that if we make a serious attempt to explicate clearly our understanding of what makes an educated person, taking care to avoid incoherence or inconsistency in our account and to complete the analysis by further analysing other concepts that form part of the definition of the original concept, and if, in addition, we take account of what are taken to be empirical facts and logical truths about other aspects of our world, we will find that some conceptions of education simply aren't tenable. Furthermore, we will see that in broad terms, we all hold the same conception.

That is to say, using my own terminology, that the criteria for proper, adequate, or good analysis are the 4 c's of clarity, coherence, completeness and compatibility (with other beliefs), and that if we meet these criteria, at least within a community where there is a substantial degree of shared belief, we shall find that we meet a fifth criterion, commonality. I would concede without argument that, whatever our concept of education, if one imagines a radically different world, then that conception might radically alter. And, of course, I am not suggesting that we all are going to agree, even within a culture, that, for example, an educated person can necessarily speak Greek. But we are going to agree that being educated is essentially a matter of developing understanding. In the world as we know it, which includes our current understanding and beliefs that we are logically incapable of ignoring while we focus on some particular question, suggestions such as that education is about being physically fit, that a quiz show champion is necessarily well educated, or that education can be equated with training or indoctrination, are all untenable.

Just as we may reasonably say that it is the case that cigarettes have a causal link with cancer, even though some people do not believe it and even though it is conceivable that in the future we shall determine that it is not the case, so we may reasonably say that it is the case that being educated is essentially a matter of developing understanding. And, proceeding from there, if we give similar careful thought to epistemology and the psychology of learning, and what matters to us as human beings in society, we may draw more specific conclusions about what education involves.

In response to those who are still impressed by the amount of undisputed data concerning actual cultural and historical differences in conception, there are three points worth making. First, the elementary point that, while it may be suggestive, no amount of evidence about the differences among people's conceptions (what they do think) can, in itself, determine the question of whether the various conceptions are all coherent (what it makes sense to think). Secondly, it is by no means clear that all such differences are, in fact, conceptual rather than the consequences of different circumstances, leading to a different particular form of the same broad concept. The view of the ancient Spartans that the young should be trained to do little more than bear arms and endure physical privation is not necessarily at variance with our view that education is primarily about developing understanding. The Spartan might agree; but given the circumstances of his world, including his understanding of what there is to be understood, this is the kind of understanding that he believes should be developed. Thirdly, we cannot do other than work on a particular problem within the terms of our broader understanding and culture. While the stronger thesis would have it that seemingly varying conceptions across cultures will turn out to be legitimately different forms of the same concept, the weaker thesis that proper analysis within a culture will lead to a common conception is sufficient for our purposes. The crucial claim here is that seeming difference of opinion as to what constitutes education amongst people who share a vast array of other concepts and beliefs, will turn out to be the product of confusion of some sort on somebody's part.

The fundamental point is that the business of analysis is not arbitrary. It is governed by rules of logic and fact. Of course, our wider belief structure may be at fault in various ways, but we cannot analyse the concept of education without reference to that belief structure. If we acknowledge that fact, it follows that rival conceptions can be evaluated by reference to their relative clarity, completeness, coherence and compatibility.

In a nutshell, the thesis emerges: notwithstanding the difficulties and degrees of tentativeness in our claim about the nature of education, it is very clear that a great deal of empirical educational research is not focused on *educational* considerations at all, and that empirical work on more specific concepts such as intelligence and critical thinking has not been convincingly shown to relate to adequate conceptions of these phenomena. The problem is not that empirical researchers never define their terms, but that even when they do, they do so by providing an operational definition without seeking in any way to justify it by reference to an explicit and full analysis. Furthermore, one may note in passing the distressing tendency for empirical researchers to be wedded to a particular type of research and consequently to operationalise the concept that is the focus of their attention in terms dictated by the research method, rather than to determine the appropriate method of research by reference to a thorough understanding of the nature of the concept, as they should.

IV. *Qualitative Research*

Much of what John Wilson has written on the topic of educational research was published when the dominant form of empirical research was what may loosely be termed quantitative. In recent years, qualitative research of various kinds has become more prevalent, which raises the question of whether this type of empirical research is subject to the same criticism.

On the face of it, one might hope that it is not. After all, part of the impetus for qualitative research was a recognition that some of the quantitative methods were inappropriate to some of the objects of inquiry and that, in particular, such methods failed to take account of the need for non-empirical interpretation and thereby distorted our understanding of various concepts and phenomena.

It is certainly the case, as the preceding argument has shown, that not all educational problems lend themselves to empirical inquiry of a quantitative kind. More generally, our respect for and the dominance of the scientific paradigm has surely led us to ignore the very real contribution to understanding the human condition that various other forms of inquiry might provide. I offer as an instance here the contribution that literature, by which I mean primarily fiction, might make to our understanding. It is true that a novel does not, generally speaking, justify its perception of the truth, but it may nonetheless provide such a perception. Secondly, it is true that the novel in itself, however convincing we find its understanding, does not provide any grounds for generalising from the particular. Thirdly, we can hardly ignore the question of how one distinguishes between the book that does illuminate the truth and one that doesn't. Nonetheless, despite these difficulties, the point that a good novel may provide more understanding than any kind of empirical research of certain kinds of issues surely remains valid.

The quality of a good novel is partly judged by reference to aesthetic criteria, or more particularly, the criteria of good writing and story telling. These considerations, however, I shall set aside as not being germane to my immediate purpose. The judgement that a novel is good is also, in many cases, partly a judgement about its verisimilitude. If we say that a particular novel about the childhood and development of an individual, such as Henry James' *Daisy Miller*, is good, then partly we are saying that it rings true. Incidentally, such a book might in some respects be very artificial, fantastical, even at one level incredible, but still illuminate certain truths. (Vladimir Nabokov's *Lolita* might be considered such an example). We are also saying that a book of this type *enhances* our understanding, in a way we find plausible, of the characters, their motivations, relationships, hopes and fears, and so forth, and thus gives us deeper insight into the human condition.

There is nothing contentious in the above paragraph. All I am pointing out is that an astute individual can depict a human situation in such a way that he increases our understanding, and that I would regard the ability to do so as one criterion of a good novelist. But it is an important point, because we seem to find it difficult to distinguish between proving something and sharpening our perception or understanding of something, while giving at least equal value to the latter. Thus, in the study of education, we spend more time on research that does indeed prove something, but not necessarily exactly what it claims to prove and not what we are actually supposed to be interested in, than we do on such things as novels that might do more to increase our understanding of the field. Furthermore, the only ways in which we can really increase our understanding of certain things, such as love, happiness, goodness, intelligence and human nature are through experience, by systematic reflection (including philosophical analysis), and through vicarious experience such as literature provides. Empirical research into happiness, for example, will always necessarily and at best be research into symptoms of our views about happiness. One cannot, logically cannot, explore the state of happiness by direct observations or directly trace causal relationships, etc. by empirical means. But one can increase one's understanding of happiness itself, both by formal reflection on the concept and by interacting with the detailed understanding of another, such as may be provided by the novelist.

It has already been conceded that trying to justify the novelist's perception as revealing is another matter, and that we do not have uniformity of opinion as to who the good novelists, in this sense, are. But we perhaps underestimate the degree of objectivity in judgement that is nonetheless possible here. In the domain of the natural sciences, we accept the notion of objectivity, because the scientific community, at any given time, agrees on various criteria that determine objectivity. The literary community is never quite as much in agreement as the scientific community, but it nonetheless remains the case that there is a degree of consistency of judgement as to the quality of various works. One may not personally like any or all authors as diverse as Trollope, Dickens, Austen, Proulx, Carol Shields, Graham Greene, William Trevor, Goethe, Elizabeth Jane Howard, Collette, Pete Dexter and D.H. Lawrence, and most of these writers may be a great deal less popular than Barbara Cartland or Agatha Christie. Yet, in terms of the verisimilitude which concerns me, it is still reasonable to contend that the former group are all good novelists. The judgement is given a degree of objectivity by the broad consensus of those who seriously immerse themselves in such works and who are thinking in terms of this criterion.

I have included these brief remarks on literature, partly because it seems to me to follow from what has been said that to increase our understanding of many aspects of the human condition, including many specifically educational concerns, we would be better employed immersing ourselves in literature than in empirical educational research. But my more immediate concern is to consider the question of whether qualitative research is in some way immune to the point made about quantitative research, namely that its quality is necessarily dependant on its philosophical underpinnings. For, it might be said, qualitative research, in that its "data are generated through interviews, written protocols, participant observation . . . self-reports" (Husen and Postlethwaite, 1994) and similar approaches, is a species of, or is very akin to, literature. The teacher telling her story, it might be concluded, is as significant as the novel.

My response to this question is that in either case the value is dependant on the implicit conceptual acumen and finesse involved. While both a good novel and a good example of qualitative research obviously depend on other factors as well, neither one can occur without clear and plausible conceptualisation, implicit or explicit, and a nose for logical connections.

While the phrase, "qualitative research," is clearly here to stay, and while it is easy to point to examples of qualitative as opposed to quantitative research, it is not, in fact, always entirely clear what the defining characteristics of qualitative research are taken to be. Superficially, one might say that quantitative research quantifies, and that it is distinguished from qualitative research in being objective rather then subjective (though the latter claim begs the question of what constitutes 'objectivity'). But a more distinguishing factor is surely that quantitative research, whatever its precise form, seeks to systematise the mode of gathering data so that it is immune to distortion occasioned by the individual perception of the researcher (s), whereas qualitative research does not. Nor is this distinction surprising, since part of the impetus to turn to a new, non-quantitative, type of research, was a misgiving that sometimes the need to systematise might be distorting the truth. Thus, for example, many have argued that systematic observation of the type pioneered in Flander's Interaction Analysis ensured a uniformity of observer interpretation, at the expense of a plausible analysis of classroom interactions. (Barrow, 1984)

Quantitative research, I am suggesting, though it also quantifies and purports to be objective, whatever its form, is distinguished by the fact that its observation procedures are systematised in the sense that they lead to uniformity of judgement: all observers will describe a particular situation in the same terms. In the purest and simplest cases, this result will be merely a function of concentrating on exclusively uncontentiously observable features, for example, whether the teacher is talking or not; in more complex cases, where it is recognised that there may be a problem of individual interpretation, observers are trained to define and hence perceive the unobservable in terms of a set of agreed observable criteria; for example, "paying attention" is defined in terms of behaviour such as "looking at the teacher". Qualitative research, by contrast, and again whatever its precise form, allows the individual observer(s) to make his/her judgement without prior agreement on observable criteria.

But it should be immediately clear that the quality of qualitative research is equally dependant on its philosophical underpinnings. The quantitative researcher can only impress us if he can distinguish between what is directly observable and what is not, if he can offer behavioural definitions that are conceptually plausible, and if he can detect logical connections and distinguish them from empirical connections. The same expectations apply to the qualitative researcher. In addition, the qualitative researcher no less than the quantitative researcher needs to provide the conceptualisation and logical reasoning that lies behind his account, if we are to be in a position to evaluate it. The quantitative researcher can usually claim that such reasoning is an automatic function of setting up and explaining his research procedures and instruments. His problem is, too often, a lack of plausibility. The qualitative researcher's problem is usually a failure to provide any such reasoning, either explicitly or implicitly.

If a novelist is good, then, by definition, he tells us something significant about human beings. By the same token, if an individual qualitative researcher is good, then, by definition he tells us something significant about whatever he is describing. But, at least at the present time, there is this enormous difference between the two enterprises: rational discourse on the quality of novelists, though far from being a science, is a well established business, whereas rational discussion on the quality of individual qualitative researchers is not. To the extent to which that is the case, to that extent a particular piece of qualitative research is beyond our appraisal.

For my immediate purposes, however, the difficulty of appraising the quality of much qualitative research is less important than the contention from which I started: no account of any educational situation, whether it be essentially descriptive or concerned with determining cause and effect, regardless of methodology, can possibly be significant except in so far as the observation is based upon clear and coherent conceptualisation and the reasoning (explanation, argument, inference, etc.) is both logical *and* available for public scrutiny. Arguments about the rival merits of different kinds of research are themselves otiose, unless they are conducted in the light of a philosophical account of the different nature of different kinds of problems.

In short, I do not see that the emergence of qualitative research has done anything in itself to solve the problem that much empirical research in education has been philosophically unsound, nor therefore to gainsay the point that philosophical sophistication is necessary to good empirical research. The logically necessary order of events remains: first, one has to articulate a clear and coherent conception of education; secondly, one has to articulate a clear and coherent conception of the central factors one is interested in; thirdly, one has to select one's investigative method(s) by reference to the nature of what one is inquiring into; fourthly, if one arrives by this process at the view that some individual account is appropriate, one needs to make explicit one's conceptual and other logical reasoning, if one is to be open to appraisal.

V. Conclusion

If the argument that John Wilson and I have presented for the crucial importance of philosophy as an underpinning and integral part of any coherent empirical research in education is sound, and if we are further correct in claiming that there is little evidence that it has in practice been appreciated, we may reasonably conclude by asking why this should be so. The case for recognising the need for philosophical analysis seems self-evident. Why can empirical researchers not see it?

Here we come to another point on which Wilson and I disagree, although as the years go by, I am coming more around to his point of view. Several years ago, at the annual meeting of the Philosophy of Education Society of Great Britain held at the University of Leicester, I first heard him make a suggestion, one amazing, even bizarre to me, that we are faced with some kind of psychopathic problem that needs to be dealt with by psychoanalysis (Wilson, 1981 and 1993). While I would now take this suggestion slightly more seriously than I did then, it leads to water in which I do not feel able and frankly have no wish to swim. But it does seem clear, since the logic of the argument is so straightforward, that we are dealing with some kind of resistance, or perhaps ignorance, rather than reasoned rejection or disagreement.

There are, I think, a number of factors that militate against taking philosophy seriously at the present time. Speaking generally, the concept of education that finds broad acceptance amongst philosophers is not much valued by those with political power, and the tolerance for reflection and theoretical study of any sort is not high, except when it is believed to lead to unequivocal solutions to practical problems. But while the climate is certainly not conducive, this circumstance does not entirely explain why empirical researchers seem unable to grasp the need for a type of analysis that they do not practice. As to that specific point, I incline to the view that *formally* empirical researchers will concede the point, but that they cannot usually act upon it, because they lack the philosophical competence and fluency that are required. This situation leads me to the practical conclusion that what is urgently needed in faculties of education is a curriculum that ensures a thorough understanding of and grounding in the nature of philosophical analysis, regardless of the specialist line of research that an individual may ultimately pursue.

It is not, after all, as if empirical researchers were claiming that logic, clarity and definition have no place in their world. The reason that they do not see that their definitions are not adequate analyses, that a clear operational definition can have the defect of being untenable as an account of a concept, that some connections are logical rather than empirical, that some claims presuppose a concept of education that bears little or no relation to education, that some issues cannot be usefully researched empirically, and that the justification for a particular type of methodology can only be located in an understanding of the object of inquiry, is not that they do not want, but that they are not able to do so, since they lack the philosophical understanding that would enable them. If we are serious about the often talked about goal of having a profession noted for its ability to reflect seriously upon practice, then we have to ensure that all practitioners, teachers and researchers, are provided with a serious understanding of philosophical analysis.

I shall conclude by noting that "serious" is a very important word in Wilson's vocabulary. Although he happens to be an engagingly unserious man, if that means that he is not solemn, sombre, gloomy or apocalyptic, he has always consistently maintained that what is largely lacking in educational theory and research is the ability to give serious (i.e. painstaking, authentic, committed, passionate, detailed, intelligent) attention to what we think we mean by what we say and do. I believe he is right.

Notes

1. Although I am using "love" only as an example here, it is worth noting that Wilson has written two books on the topic (Wilson, 1965 and 1980)
2. I coined and explained the term "degree word" in Barrow, 1980. (See also Barrow and Milburn, 1990)
3. The interview was broadcast by CBC on August 19th. Hana Gartner spoke with Professor Hare of the University of British Columbia.

References

Barrow, R. (1976) *Common Sense and the Curriculum.* (London: Allen and Unwin).
(1980) *Happiness.* (Oxford: Martin Robertson).
(1981) *The Philosophy of Schooling.* (Brighton, Sussox: Wheatsheaf).
(1983) "Does the question, what is education?, make sense?" *Educational Theory* 33, 191 – 195.
(1984) *Giving Teaching Back to Teachers.* (Brighton, Sussex: Wheatsheaf.
(1985) "Misdescribing a cow: the question of conceptual correctness" *Educational Theory* 35, 205 – 207.
(1990) *Understanding Skills: Thinking, Feeling and Caring.* (London, Ont.: Althouse Press).
(1993) *Language, Intelligence and Thought.* (Aldeshot, Harts: Edward Elgar).

Barrow, R. & Milburn, G. (1990) *A Critical Dictionary of Educational Concepts,* 2nd Edition (London: Harvester Wheatsheaf).

Husen, T. & Postlethwaite, T.N. (1994) *International Encyclopedia of Education*, 2nd Edition (Oxford: Pergamon).

Phillips, D.C. (1976) *Holistic Thought in Social Science.* (California: Stanford University Press).
(1987) *Philosophy, Science and Social Inquiry.* (Oxford: Pergamon).

Searle, J.R. (1992) *The Rediscovery of the Mind.* (Cambridge, Mass: MIT Press).
(1995) *The Construction of Social Reality* (Harmondsworth: Allen Lane).

Singer, P. (1995) *Rethinking Life and Death* (New York: St. Martin's Press).

Wilson, J. (1965) *Logic and Sexual Morality.* (Harmondsworth: Penguin Books).
(1966) *Equality.* (London: Hutchinson).
(1968) *Education and the Concept of Mental Health.* (London: Routledge and Kegan Paul).

(1972) *Philosophy and Educational Research.* (Slough: NFER).
(1975) *Educational Theory and the Preparation of Teachers.* (Slough: NFER)
(1977) *Philosophy and Practical Education.* (London: Routledge and Kegan Paul).
(1979) *Fantasy and Common Sense in Education* (Oxford: Martin Robertson).
(1980) *Love, Sex and Feminism.* (New York: Praeger).
(1981) "Concepts, Contestability and the Philosophy of Education," *Journal of Philosophy of Education*, Vol.15, No. 1.
(1985) "The Inevitability of Certain Concepts (including Education)," *Educational Theory*, Vol. 35, No. 2.
(1986) *What Philosophy Can Do.* (London: Macmillan).
(1993) *Reflection and Practice.* (London, Ont.: Althouse Press).

The Basis of Education

Chapter Six

John Wilson and the Basis of Education

Spencer J. Maxcy

For many American university students in the 1960's and 1970's, their introduction to philosophy, done in the British style, was John Wilson's small text, *Thinking With Concepts*. The fact that it was first published in 1963, and yet can be read today with such richness, illustrates something of Wilson's legacy. John Wilson followed this little text with a steady stream of published books and articles to form a central contribution to the literature of educational philosophy.

From within the "ordinary language" analysis movement, Wilson has offered the unique gift of promoting a reasoned discourse grounded in a moral vision for all education. Wilson has successfully shown how thinking may be both an everyday activity, as well as a refined and professionally astute practice. More than any of his contemporaries, Wilson offered us ready guidance in the techniques of reasoning, a focused seriousness regarding the enormous number of confusing concepts and arguments in education, and demonstrable models of moral reflection.

Perhaps John Wilson's most precious gift was himself, as a model and a teacher. He often admonished students that more philosophy can be learned "punting on the river" than in any classroom. Generations of Oxford students and visitors learned from him how to be more passionate and reasoned in their daily lives. Wilson made philosophy a public activity which allowed all sorts of non-traditional learners to enter the discourse of reason and repudiation. It was through this approach that arcane philosophy became understandable to the teacher, administrator, student and parent.

The purpose of this essay is to probe John Wilson's thought, so that we may consider what counts as the basis of his teaching. This ground supports the scaffold universe of his fuller philosophy, lending meaning to his conception of education. To this end, we shall explore what he may take to be involved in asking the question, What is the basis of education? In seeking to answer this query, it may prove important to both examine his conceptions of 'ideology', 'authority', 'democracy', 'leadership' and 'morality', and to attempt to nest his views within a political, philosophic tradition by contrasting this to other traditions. In passing, we may be able to locate the unique moral character of his reasoning. It is this latter feature of Wilson's philosophy that has been most appealing, yet elusive, for so many readers.

Philosophy

John Wilson begins his *Thinking With Concepts*, a book written for British school children, with talk of a new "technique of thought" which could be applied over a wide field; "the analysis of concepts," he called it (vii-viii). He proceeds to outline techniques and how they might apply to concepts in everyday life, raising the proper questions about fact and meaning, about avoiding temperamental difficulties and about engaging in the techniques of analysis themselves. Wilson highlights the importance of isolating questions of concept, avoiding the trap of single "right answers", exploring cases of use of concepts, and becoming conscious of social context and considering psychological anxiety (23 – 37). It is important to note that Wilson finds the consequences of good analysis to be a more clearly understood language, and not changed practice. This point is significant, and we shall return to it later.

Because John Wilson's work is in philosophy, any effort to explicate or critique his writings requires a skeletal schema of key concepts and meanings. Hence, in attempting to set forth Wilson's 'concepts', whether it be of the basis of education or anything else, it is important to read what he wrote of the notion 'concept'. Doing this may reveal the fact that his criteria for what makes a concept meaningful pulls in larger elements of his philosophic foundation. For example, his use of the concept of 'democracy' carries with it criterial conditions that must be met for us to count it as "having, using, and acquiring a concept" (Wilson, 1972, 73). Far from being commonsensical about concepts and their use in arguments, Wilson is very careful to mark off a conception that is fruitful from one that is merely the "psychologist's efforts to explain it to us" (Wilson, 1972, 72).

It would come as no surprise to anyone familiar with his writings that John Wilson's foundations for education and his philosophy contain rich threads drawn from Utilitarianism, Ordinary Language Analysis and British school experiences. His characterizing marks are: a brilliant philosophic acumen clothed in a common sense approach, a dedication to "serious" philosophic dialogue, a desire to develop "a general methodology" by which confusing concepts and arguments may be disentangled, and a deep and abiding respect for all persons with whom he comes into contact. His style of philosophizing is neither ivory-towerish nor pedestrian. Through easy-flowing speech and hearty examples, he raises the standard of a new philosophy around which anyone really interested in the problems and prospects of education and schooling must rally.

In the dissection of Wilson's many contributions to the ongoing discourse surrounding how philosophy works, I argue that his writings necessarily aid us in developing a saner world of school practice, especially in view of the near chaotic cultural conditions found operative in this *fin de le siecle*. It is difficult to know where to begin an analysis of the contributions of this prolific and insightful writer who has covered such subjects as mental health, sexuality, theology and education. It is difficult to identify a core set of Wilson beliefs, for he purposely leads us to think for ourselves. His "post-holes" are easy to follow, yet he may be best read where he applies his ideas to unique problems and issues. One task of this essay is to locate John Wilson's philosophical foundations, and I wish to start in the arena where Wilson firmly denies such foundations exist: the political.

Ideology and Liberalism

Many philosophers, like Marx and Dewey, have tethered their philosophy to some political belief system. They have rooted their philosophic views, and coincidentally formed the raw underbelly of their conception of education, in the rich soil of political culture and the experience of disenfranchisement or repression, on the one hand, or power and privilege, on the other. Yet, while some philosophers offer strong versions of political humanism as their fundamental grounding for education (Barber, 1984; Selznick, 1992; Cherryholmes, 1988; Bernstein, 1983), others, like John Wilson, regard the political dimension as a necessary component, but also a dangerous foundation upon which to build a systematic philosophy of education.

All of politics quickly reduces itself to what Wilson might call 'ideology'. The negative connotation of ideology may thus steer us away from it entirely. Wilson's foundation or basis of education is found, not in the political state and its founding fathers, but in human reason and the public dialogue that must exercise that capacity. Yet, if ideology is the antithesis of the kind of free ranging intelligence Wilson champions, what must the non-political base be? Even more, what conditions must be met such that education may be conducted for the good, if good is not a socio-political way of living?

The answer to these questions brackets John Wilson's philosophy and aids in understanding its reference to sources in British linguistic philosophic traditions. It also illustrates the worth-making condition which must be met as a context that allows for the full and free use of reasoned thinking. The essential vision which John Wilson's philosophy of the group must embrace is built up out of a kind of discursive liberalism, not the liberalism of John Dewey or other "democrats," but rather more like the liberalism of intelligent minds. But, like Dewey, Wilson is committed to a gradualism, not a revolutionary approach, to changing the contextual features that support education. He is at his best, like Dewey, when he is speaking of the mode of inquiry, education and experiment in determining the best ways to solve specific conflicts and disagreements (Dewey, 1916). This is not to say that Wilson is a pragmatist, for this he is not; rather, we see in his writings an effort to specify the 'practical requirements' to be met in any inquiry, and to illustrate a 'seriousness' appropriate to the task. Like his fellow liberals, he employs a critical reason to solve concrete problems of practice. Hence, the first support leg of John Wilson's philosophy and basis of education is human reason; and the confusion over linguistic meaning is sufficiently ended by a restoration of meaning, and not changed practice.

At the opposite end of the pole of the modern liberal state, John Wilson finds doctrinaire thinking of any kind to be a prime evil. It is the nature of this counter-context which he refers to as ideological. Of course, as Selznik (1992) tells us, 'ideology' is a vague concept: ". . . a set of explicit and coherent beliefs about values and social reality" (409). Ideology may be contrasted with 'civility', or a genuine communal consensus. Here the expression of a cultural identity may interfere with a personal freedom to pursue a practice. Freedom of choice comes into conflict with the community's interest in vindicating its beliefs, particularly where there are reasons set forth (Selznik, 408). He proceeds to call for "a threshold standard of critical morality," by which he has in mind a criterial boundary condition or set of conditions, somewhere between a positive civility on its way to destroying individual freedoms and a negative or pathological ideology.

'Ideology', as a matter of definition, ". . . says nothing about distortion, exclusiveness, psychic coercion, or overreaching" (Selznik, 409). We may have nothing to say about a liberal or conservative ideology. Something more is needed to locate the deeper meaning attached to 'ideology' in our ordinary vocabulary.

Ideologies speak for groups, articulating in various degrees of completeness, the interests of the group. For example, the women's liberation ideology purports to speak for women, Marxist communism speaks for the working class, and so forth. Ideologies play an important role in group life as they seek to raise consciousness of such groups, and encourage individual members of the group "to feel a sense of shared identity and fate" (Selznik, 410).

Thus, it is possible to argue that any philosophic position, including Wilson's, may be located within an ideology. Yet, as Wilson rightly points out, we may find the ideology either acceptable or unacceptable based upon its possibilities of warranting our own particular point of view.

Authority and Rules

While ideology may function as the antipode of reasoned self-governance, for Wilson, it is nonetheless essential to accept authority. The difficulty is to separate an authority, in the sense of authoritarian, from an authority that is righteous rule-governing. There is 'authority', and there is Authority. The second leg of Wilson's support basis for education is located in the concept of authority.

Lukes (1987) correctly points out that the question of what is authority is really two questions. The one is an analytical question and seeks to identify the elements of the concept of authority: how these are structured, how the criteria may be specified such that we may recognize the possession, exercise, the acceptance of authority, and how it may differ from other forms of influence. The second question is the normative one: how we define legitimate authority, how we see an authority to be worthy of acceptance, and how we determine what kinds of utterances are to be deemed authoritative. John Wilson treats both questions, and thus moves beyond the boundaries of traditional analytic philosophy. I believe it is this boldness that enjoins us to John Wilson's work.

Wilson (1977) couples authority with the criterion of rule-following. He writes: "Anything that could seriously be called a 'society' or 'social group'. . . involves some kind of interaction between its members. . . that they engage in some rule-following activity . . ." (49-50). However, Wilson goes on to say that ". . . any overall or *a priori* preference for a particular style or regime—'authoritarian', 'democratic', or whatever— is likely to be doctrinaire" (56). The type of arrangement depends, Wilson tells us, on "*what sort of transaction* we wish to take place, or what kind of business we want to conduct, what the purposes are . . ." (56). It is this practical transactive quality of the authority that makes it worthwhile or not.

Rules are vital for authority to work, Wilson maintains. Additionally, a ". . . breach of these rules must, at least characteristically if not in every case, be taken to entail the enforcement of some disadvantage on the breaker . . ." (59). Wilson proceeds to clarify what he means by disadvantage and how it relates to 'punishment', but the tone of his remarks remains the same. He contrasts his notion of a society of human beings with that of Kant's community of angels. Against this ideal community, Wilson posts a society of non-angelic, "bloody-minded" individuals who need ". . . decision-procedures and authorities. . . ," so that they may "exchange goods, play cricket, hold debates, run railways, or whatever . . ." (53). In the final analysis, "authorities (referees, arbitrators, umpires, etc.) are necessary, not just to punish vice, but to provide clarity in those rule-governed activities. . ." (53).

Yet, authority must be also a matter of perspective (Lukes, 1987). We may view the authority transaction from the side of the person in authority, from the side of those who are subject to this authority, or from a third, outsider, perspective. In addition, as Lukes tells us, authority may be seen from the standpoint of someone who looks at the authority relations from above, and notes how they relate to social norms and standards (something like a court judge would do).

Wilson moves through some of these perspectives, to the claim that ". . . 'unquestioned obedience' is required by the very notion of authority." Although he adds that questions will arise about the legitimacy of authorities, their scope, form and methods by which they operate, and so forth (55); it is the case that even when we question authority we ". . . are involved in obeying rules" (56). He seems to favor the perspective of the person in authority, and the judge who stands outside of the authority relations. Wilson seems not to be overly sensitive to the interests of those who are subject to authority. This oversight is best exemplified in his discussion of teaching.

Within the educational sector, Wilson's proposal to teachers' relative authority is for them to rely on their common sense. To this end, they must be concerned: (1) that the authority must be exercised so that learning can take place, (2) that the authority is clearly defined and enforced properly and (3) that, ideally, the rules are inherent in what is being learned (56).

The crucial problem facing Wilson is how a system that warrants reasoned inquiry (philosophic mind) may at once rest upon rules, yet avoid becoming an ideology. The answer emerges in the form of "the expert leader."

Leadership and Democracy

If we allow the form of social organization to float relative to the enterprise carried on within, we are open to alternative authorities, various kinds of rules, and hence alternative modes of leadership. Indeed Wilson recognizes that captains are needed for ships, generals for armies, and so forth. In addition, having established a decade earlier the fact that morality is moral reasoning and, hence, a learned skill, he and Cowell (1983) write that some people are "just better at politics or indeed morality . . ." (113) They go on to argue that "leaders ought to be chosen on the basis of their expertise, and on other bases (although ultimately they should be accountable to all of us)" (114).

Rather than argue for the primacy of a regime or mode of social organization such as 'democracy' (recall these are 'ideological' for Wilson), there is a stress placed on philosophic-mindedness, a reasonableness connected with extant, plural epistemologies, and an elite of "better" governors being placed in leadership roles (Wilson & Cowell, 14). In 1963, Wilson had already expressed his dissatisfaction with democracy. Writing in *Thinking With Concepts*, he illustrates how in conducting analysis, a mixed question has no right answer. However, his illustration is about 'democracy'. He winds up saying that if the criteria for the word, 'democracy', as a satisfactory method of government, could be tied to a country's budget being balanced by popular vote, rather than through the acts of acknowledged experts, ". . . then in that sense of 'democracy' it's obviously not very satisfactory, because it makes for instability" (25).

Exactly twenty years later, Wilson wrote a devastating critique of the concept of 'democracy', declaring "democracy is a myth" (Wilson & Cowell, 1983). In this essay, Wilson and his co-author, offer their definition of 'democracy' as simple majority rule, and then challenge it by arguing that an expert ruler is surely better than an ignorant majority. But this move reduces democracy to mere decision-making.

Adopting an argument strongly reminiscent of political philosopher Robert Dahl, Wilson and Cowell say experts exist, in the sense that there are "people better equipped than others to decide what is right, in the context of ends as well as means, for a society or a state" (1971, 34). Granted that such "experts" are not entitled to enforce their status as experts or their decisions upon society, it would be wise for us to entrust such decisions to them nonetheless. The authors further defend this view by saying that lunatics and children ought not to be regarded as such political experts, but beyond these cases, it is easy for us to identify who these experts may be. Thus, the third leg of Wilson's philosophy is 'leadership', and more particularly for education, it is the leadership of learned individuals, or expert authorities.

Wilson goes on to say that there are some standard interests and needs that are common among all human beings, that not everyone is aware of these, and that political experts have a greater understanding of what people need, as opposed to what they *want*. The conclusion is that the political expert can tell us what is in our own best interest, while we are only aware of what we want. This view is reminiscent of the position of elitist democracy theorists in the U.S. who sought to protect the people from the different policy choices that needed to be made.

By way of criticism of this kind of argument, it might be pointed out that needs come to be equated with what makes people *happy*. This is a utilitarian assumption which today's citizens can no longer make. There are things we may need, in the sense of 'should have', which will not make us happy (either in the short or the long run). The idea that political experts know what is best for us (meet our needs), seems to be countered by the evidence. First, the individuals most affected by a political decision are the first source of evidence as to whether it is a need or a want. Secondly, the decision to make a want a need, or vice versa, is too often the arbitrary decision of political office holders who are bending to certain interest groups.

A couple of cases seem to bear this out. Do Americans need assault weapons in their homes? The politicos in Washington say they do. But they are yielding to the American Rifle Association, and their campaign funding is heavily supported by this interest group. Therefore, it is the wants of the political expert which are being served in this instance. Year after year, in the educational sector, educational programs for the disadvantaged are neglected or under funded by the U.S. Congress. There is demonstrable need for some of these special programs, but the political leadership simply fails to see their importance until it is brought to their attention by special interest groups. The history of Special Education in the U.S. is an example of this oversight. Only when a small group of parents of physically and mentally challenged children and youth lobbied Congress did legislation pass to address these special needs (Ravitch, 1983, 307 – 311).

The notion that leaders ought to be selected for their political expertise resembles Plato's injunction that a clique of "philosopher kings" rule the Republic. We are cautioned that we ought not follow the lead of Plato and place our "money on one specific regime" (Wilson & Cowell, 116). Nevertheless, implicit in their recommendation is that we use political leadership as a teaching model, allowing children to imitate leaders. That these leaders are to be knowledge experts rather than poets or artists seems to follow. Aesthetic interests are not specified as they would be served in political leadership.

If we examine the concept of human nature at work in this account of leadership, we find that leaders are special kinds of people. These special political experts run the risk of not rising to the top in an ideological setting. Thus, Wilson, in part, is critical of ideology where it prevents knowledge experts from gaining control, or where it allows "certain types of people" the venue to "feel powerful" (Wilson & Cowell, 114).

Even the popular method of electing leaders may be wrong, according to Wilson and Cowell. The claim is made: "No serious business or other organization would choose a leader by the sort of public methods which seem to apply for selecting presidents of the USA, or emperors in the later Roman Republic." (Wilson & Cowell, 114). Hence, popular vote and democratic consensus are viewed as suspicious, owing to the fact that the non-expert may gain office and power.

Against this view of leadership, a large literature exists which supports the view that today, school leadership is entirely given over to rational-technical management, lacking any kind of moral-ethical sensitivity. This view has been reviewed elsewhere (Maxcy, 1991; 1995). Wilson's recommendation would lead to a desire for even more of such technical skill at the expense of democratic participation in the schools. Leadership takes precedence over participation. Democracy is reduced to a style of administration. Getting things done correctly or reasonably assumes paramount importance. Groups, because they are groups, cannot do much better than enlightened leaders.

Looking more deeply into the position advanced, we find a classical liberal position. The position has it that the best people rise to the surface and become administrators, if allowed; that somehow public and private distinctions must be kept intact; that fraternity is somehow rather meaningless, or at least, it is not as important as governing well; that equality must never be sacrificed to excellence; and, that somehow merit is ultimately bestowed.

Moral Thinking on a High Ground

The pivotal point upon which the basis or foundation of Wilson's educational philosophy rotates is his notion of the moral. For an analyst, the form of reason which attends the moral is a necessary condition for any serious examination of society's institutions. By his "moral point of view" is meant the following: for reason to be of any significance, it must be sensitive to the moral-ethical dimension of human action and the social group arena wherein this action takes place.

It is no surprise that Wilson dedicates so many of his books to students and teachers; for they are operating at the beginning of moral sense. In his book, *Moral Thinking: A Guide for Students,* he faults us for our lack of serious consideration of thinking. He tells us that many times we are apt not to see thinking as useful because it may not have an immediate payoff. In addition, we are tempted to solve problems quickly or simply to escape from them. We use a wide variety of substitutes for thinking, Wilson points out.

Wilson seeks to spell out a methodology for moral thought by specifying what thinking involves, i.e. respect for language, for facts and for established branches of knowledge (Wilson, 1973). But, there are different types of thinking. For Wilson, 'morality' is defined as a form of thinking, similar to but distinct from, other forms of thinking such as scientific, historical or literary. He cautions us that thinking must be done in the open, holding up ideas for public inspection. Thinking about morals and religion is different and necessarily leads to questions about meaning, and such thinking is not done through books alone.

Wilson touches on the ideological issue once again when he speaks of the necessity for rooting his moral thinking within the framework of a liberal society rather than a totalitarian one. But he hesitates to call this regime 'democratic'. However, rules and contracts are essential within this framework, he argues (Wilson, 1973).

Having a moral belief, Wilson asserts, is not just having a certain feeling or intuitively grasping it as moral; rather it is holding *reasons* for claiming some issue as moral. Hence, Wilson distances himself from moral intuitionists, on the one hand, and caring theorists, on the other. Moral action is tied to rationality. Being "good" at morality means that you stick to laws of logic, use language correctly and attend to facts (Wilson, 1973, 39).

R.M. Hare echoes Wilson's sentiments regarding the moral point of view when he argues that, "naturalism has a great deal to be said for it, especially as an account of the intuitive level of moral thinking and of the moral concepts used at that level" (Hare, 68 – 69). Hare correctly points out that the way to discover canons of moral reasoning is to study the meanings of moral words. By searching the linguistic conventions of a people, it would be possible to locate what moral meanings they had affixed to words. However, this descriptive task is insufficient for both Wilson and Hare because it could lead to the ". . . mistake of confusing moral with linguistic conventions . . ." (69).

Wilson is a moral reformer, and, therefore, cannot be a supporter of received moral notions as such. Anthropology is helpful, but it is not a reformer's science for either Hare or Wilson. Native verbal agreement on 'right' or 'moral' is not enough. A moral anthropology is blind-sided to Hare's maxim: "No substantial disagreement without verbal agreement"

(69). Thus, Wilson's final leg for his philosophy and philosophy of education is the moral.

Conclusions

John Wilson's concept of education rests upon the bedrock of moral reasoning, eschews ideology where it contorts such rational discourse, and embraces liberalism where it supports and protects the right to such thought and directs the point of such thinking to a fundamental understanding of the ideas that drive our social institutions and our lives.

Wilson rightly sensitizes us to the view that philosophy, as it informs moral thinking, has a larger role to perform. As part of a reflective perspective on moral-ethical discourse/practice, we must seek a reflective morality which has an eye upon communicative processes (discussion and debate), but also an eye toward the social relationships and undergirding power that supports those webs of social transactions.

The resources of any moral-ethical methodology are necessarily rooted in the social facts of the context, and here ideology is not necessarily an evil. In the affirmative and proactive desire to build a positive quality through action, a moral method that posits itself as *res gentes* and as dedicated to an aesthetic quest for building quality is needed.

The basis of John Wilson's philosophy and his conception of education rests on four fundamental ideas: reason, rule-authority, leadership and morality. When joined, these notions underwrite the philosophic mind as it utilizes methods of inquiry aimed at serious consideration of the rule-authorities or leadership required for good people to prosper in a collective state. To lead well is to be simultaneously moral-ethical in attitude and practice.

Finally, perhaps no one in the second half of the 20th century has done more to re-direct the realm of educational problems and issues toward reasoned inquiry and discussion than John Wilson. Those who have known his work, had the privilege to watch him in the classroom, and count John as a friend, are indeed the fortunate ones of the philosophic community.

References

Anderson, Charles W. (1990) *Pragmatic Liberalism.* Chicago: University of Chicago Press.

Bernstein, Richard J. (1983) *Beyond Objectivism and Relativism: Science Hermeneutics, and Praxis.* Philadelphia: University of Pennsylvania Press

Dewey, John (1916) *Democracy and Education.* New York: McMillan.

Hare, R.M. (1981) *Moral Thinking: Its Levels, Method and Point.* Oxford: Clarendon Press

Lukes, Steven (1987) "Perspectives on Authority," in *Authority Revisted.* Nomos XXIX. Edited by J. Roland Pennock and John W. Chapman. New York University Press, 59 – 75

Maxcy, Spencer J. (1991) *Educational Leadership: A Critical Prag-matic Perspective* New York: Bergin and Garvey.
(1995) *Democracy, Chaos and the New School* Thousand Oaks, CA: Corwin Press

Ravitch, Diane (1983) *The Troubled Crusade: American Education 1945 – 1980.* New York: Basic Books.

Selznick, Philip (1992) *The Moral Commonwealth: Social Theory and the Promise of Community* Berkeley, CA: University of California Press

Wilson, John (1961) *Reason and Morals* Cambridge University Press, Cambridge
(1963) *Thinking With Concepts.* Cambridge: Cambridge University Press
(1971) "Politics and Expertise," *Philosophy* 96 (75), 34 –37
(1973) *Moral Thinking: A Guide for Students.* London: Heinemann
(1972) *Philosophy and Educational Research* Windsor, England: National Foundation For Educational Research in England and Wales

(1977)   *Philosophy and Practical Education* London; Routledge & Kegan Paul

(1983)   "The Democratic Myth," with Barbara Cowell. *Journal Of Philosophy of Education.* 17 (1), 111 – 117

Love and Personal Relationships

Chapter Seven

෨෬

All You Need Is Love?

Charles Brock

John Wilson's *Love Between Equals* is a delight to read and ponder. His mind runs in high gear, and reading him is not unlike hearing Wilson talk. He loves a good discussion, and, if he cannot find it with others, John launches one with himself. John Wilson is witty and profound at raising old questions with new insights, and he comes to some useful ideas on how to live our lives. In fact, he has raised fundamental points about love.

In doing so, Wilson is refreshingly old-fashioned in that he mixes disciplines. It is anybody's guess why we got ourselves into the trap of specialization. Perhaps there is too much to read now. But the result of this is that we have truncated ourselves dreadfully by not venturing out of our chosen areas of study. Oxford can be one of the worst places for this. "Not my period" is commonly said when a don is asked to comment on some major problem which affects us all, such as the Common Market. Even though we sit together in meetings and meals, there isn't much talk on the 'big' subjects such as love. We compartmentalize ourselves and dig our own burrows with our friends. But John Wilson does no such thing. He philosophizes, theologizes, psychologizes and quotes literature and personal stories to mix together. It is a delightful brew, and it should be the ideal of every university. The Greeks knew how to do it, and maybe that is where John learned it. Would that there were more like him and that Oxford could become an Athens once again.

What about his ideas on love? It goes without saying that love among equals has many paradoxical aspects. It is something most of us have or want because of the benefits it brings, but it also causes no end of pain. Love may be a "many-splendoured thing," but it can also be a "stake in the heart" that causes no end of trouble.

Most people know of the problems. *"Jealousy, rage, love, ecstasy— just keep telling yourself it's only an opera"* was the content of an advertisement close to life that I noticed recently. Love can bring out, rather than suppress, the excessive neediness which is linked to personal instability; it can foster anger and lead to revenge; and it often is partial and narrow in its interests to the exclusion of the rest of the world and even one's best interests.

Yet everybody seems to want it; there is much talk about it; others write about it; some actually do it; some give up on it. Many people assume that it will solve all their problems—"all you need is love"—and are bitterly disappointed as time goes by. Love is crooned endlessly on the radio, analysed on telly talk shows, causes money to flow into magazines and agony aunts, and is poured over by those being analysed and their analysts. People will pay hugely for love, either in material, psychological or spiritual terms. It is even discovered at some Oxford colleges. John Wilson gets some of us going on this topic as we bolt down our food and guzzle our wine [for such, it seems, are Oxford customs not to spend too long with each other]. We may get indigestion from talking about love, if not from fast eating. Most avoid the philosophical corner of High Table, hoping to sleep sounder than the argumentative and frustrated love crunchers.

What does John Wilson say about love between equals? There is much here to summarize, but I will only be able to discuss a few points which I see as some of his key ideas. He claims:

A. Love is the child of want or need. As Aristotle said, the lover is half a whole without the other. Thus there is the desire to share oneself fully in order to become whole. One finds pleasure in the love object, is strongly attached to him/her in mind and heart, and wishes to preserve it with a permanent intensity of desire and attachment, not manipulating, but truly sharing. It is not something about B that A wants, but B itself, unlike Plato who uses lovers to get to "higher" things. The lover willingly gratifies the other's desires. Living together with another means a total partnership and sharing of oneself with the other. Affection and justice are central in all this. Love is unitary and ought not to be divided up, though it does have various features. Love wants the whole person, not their different parts and not for what they might represent in some larger good. Total sharing is the key to love.

Treating others as equals involves taking their wants or preferences seriously, not 'what is good for them'. Here the Golden Rule works. "Do unto others as you would like others to do to you." This can refer to bed as well as board, to ideas as well as laughter or tears.

B. This isn't the self-denying love that it might appear to be. It is mutually self-regarding and not simply self-giving as agape often claims to be. Agape prohibits true sharing. It is aloof and above the battle of life, thin and impersonal. It is a non-starter for close personal relationships. Wilson writes, "Try to be married to a saint." Like God, s/he doesn't really need anyone. Agape amputates our needs and desires, but these are parts of the self that need to be there. God, Mother Theresa, St. Francis and Jesus, etc. stood alone, isolated from others and deep personal relationships. That is why monks and nuns are to be celibate. That is the only way they can be celibate, but it is an inadequate form of love.

C. Problems of sex and aggression will always be with us, but can and should be worked out, redeemed or sublimated in close, loving relationships. Religions, like Christianity, foundered on these twin rocks. Moralizing certainly won't solve anything, though psychotherapy can help when it is based on re-parenting to replace the losses that happened in childhood.

I will offer some reflections on these parts of John Wilson's work, and see how they develop after inflicting them with some of my germs.

Love's Endurance

John Wilson discusses Plato on love and disagrees with him on a crucial matter. Plato claims that human love is a means to an end. In his seminal work on love, the *Symposium*, Plato states that the lover moves around the different stages of beauty, beginning with physical and spiritual love, passing through the laws, and eventually reaching up to knowledge and the everlastingly beautiful. This journey was popular with the later mystics. John Wilson isn't happy with this view, as indeed many people aren't today. They want to have love between equals worthy in its own right and for its own sake, not love of some quality in or about the person. They also feel that mutual love is diminished if it is only a stage on life's way or a ladder toward perfection.

But there might be good reason for finding love between equals as a means to an end, and it might even help with our mutual relations. Over concentration on the lover or even family might help cause their downfalls. It is not only the problem that we might expect too much from ourselves, but also we might feed off each other and end up consuming the lover. This often happens and leads to the breakdown of many relationships today. We need goals that are bigger than ourselves in order to get our lives into perspective. So, when the troubles come with love, and they are bound to happen, we have more on which to fall back or more toward which to strive than what our partners or other close relationships can give us. We need bigger, wider goals to foster and conserve the love among equals.

This is the argument from Western religions (Judaism, Christianity, Islam) which clearly stake out a claim that love between equals isn't enough on which to build a life, nor can it be the *telos* of life. An unequal love comes first, and that is love for God. This preference is clear in the command, "Hear, O Israel, the Lord our God is One, and you shall love the Lord your God with all your heart, mind, etc." Jesus inserts another Old Testament verse to complete his Great Commandment, "you shall love your neighbor as yourself." Until recently, even the purposes of marriage put children, community values and the remedy for lust at a higher level than the love for the spouse [cf 1662 Anglican Prayer Book Order for Marriage]. In Victorian times, marriage was a means for procreation, and the paterfamilias rarely chose his wife as a soul mate. There is also the rather unpopular notion these days that we are part of a society that is more than a collection of individuals. I realize this view isn't good conservative party, political doctrine at present, but it is good sociology and religion. Just as family can and should affect how we think and relate, so can society.

Everybody talks about the crisis of marriage these days. There are many books and advice centers that try to help. Indeed there are a number of academics who specialize in this, and well they may. With something like half of the marriages breaking up, we need careful and thoughtful analyses. A Sunday paper gave the following bits of advice to maintain a good marriage, based on research by a number of specialists:

> Romance and passion are less important than mutual goodwill and the feeling of being 'in this together'
> Compromise—and understand what makes your partner tick.
> Stick to the point in rows and don't character assassinate.
> Talk about what you value in each other.
> Don't cheat.
> Detach emotionally from your childhood family.

(*Independent*, London, 30 June 1996)

It is interesting to note that nothing is said about having higher goals, although they quoted Jack Dominion, one of the most respected writers on marriage in Britain, without giving his views that religious faith is helpful to any marriage in that it brings mutual goals that are beyond the constraints and limitations of personalities.

What I am arguing here is that we have something to gain from the Greek and Hebrew ideas of love that go beyond good advice, but begin to set out goals and ideals, including but transcending, mutual love. These goals and ideals make love between equals actually work. Can I give an example of what it means to find a relationship, within a framework that overarches the personal, but makes those involved bigger than they might have been on their own? I am interested in biblical characters because I preach and teach about them on a regular basis. So I have formed a close relationship with a few of them.

Central to the Old Testament is the rather dysfunctional family of Moses, Aaron and Miriam. Aaron created the Golden Calf, much to the unsympathetic fury of Moses. Miriam criticised Moses for being dictatorial and marrying a Cushite [black?] second wife. The love which these family members share with each other is not recorded, maybe deliberately. Presumably they acted like many brothers and sisters living together. Moses is fascinating. Freud chased him all over the Bible in order to try to get at the root of a number of problems such as the origins of Israel, the relation of the leader to the followers, the concept of sacrifice, the origins of religion and monotheism and the persecution of the Jews. In 1995, I organized an Oxford seminar on the use of the exodus traditions in Judaism, Christianity and Islam, using this rather unholy family as an example of how you can still do big things together, but not get along very well. That's the point of the example. You don't need to be especially happy with each other to work together for a bigger goal, such as they did in freeing Israel from servitude, instituting a new constitution and arriving at a new land. That was quite an achievement.

Though we can only guess, there must have been some kind of mutuality and sense of achievement in what they were able to do as a family. If I could do a fraction of that with my family, I suspect we would love each other better in spite of our many contradictions and differences.

Love's Expense

C.S. Lewis mentions the occasion when William Morris wrote a poem called "Love Is Enough," and a reviewer said briefly, "It isn't."

But why not? There are libraries on this. Classical and modern discussions abound. Part of the trouble is that we have limited views of love. We need to distinguish types of love, or aspects of love, within the one. The Greeks had many words for it. As a rough guide, *ego* is self love; *eros* is the desire for another, but it can also focus on non-human qualities such as truth, beauty, God; *stergo* is affection such as parents to offspring, people for their ruler, dogs for their masters, etc.; *philia* might be called strong, but tender, feelings for friends; and *agape* is self-giving love without expectation for reward. These are brief definitions which could be expanded a great deal. There has always been much debate about whether we can divide up love into various parts or whether it is unitary. John Wilson wants to unite eros and philia, but leave out agape when it comes to vital and lasting personal relationships.

I too want to claim that we have much to gain from Plato's concept of eros. If we take eros to be "desire" that is not only sexual, but also includes desire for God, the true, good and beautiful as well as for other human beings and animals, then we have a more balanced view of love and of the possibilities of what a loving God is like. We can love God "erotically" for what he is, for her qualities of goodness and beauty, not just for the sake of duty. The mystics always knew about this response.

Perhaps the most telling criticism of love in the New Testament is its lack of interest in erotic love between individuals such as is given in the delectable *Song of Songs* in the Old Testament. That is not the case in

All You Need Is Love?

some of the Gnostic gospels. One suspects the reason that they never made it into the biblical canon is because of the suspicion about physical love held by parts of the early church.

> ... the companion of the [Saviour is] Mary Magdelene. [But Christ loved] her more than [all] the disciples and used to kiss her [often] on her [mouth]. The rest of [the disciples were often offended by it . . .]. They said to him, 'Why do you love her more than all of us?' The Saviour answered and said to them, 'Why do I not love you as [I love] her?'
> (From the *Gospel of Philip* quoted in *The Gnostic Gospels*, Elaine Pagels, Penguin, London, 1990, p. 84).

There are also problems with agape, and they need to be seen for what they are. Analyses by Wilson and Freud help us to see some of the problems, especially if agape is used as the one and only allowable form of love or, if misunderstood, is the cause of cold, truncated, amputated, dutiful detachment that is such a frost. But I wonder if more is needed for our lives together than ego, eros, stergo and philia. Why not add agape, but mix it with the others so we have a fizzler cocktail? The forms of love can remain separate, but intertwined. An analogy would be a tree that supports vines that give wine, but the vines do not suck the sap from the stem of the tree. Wilson strolls by a good example whenever he walks on Mansfield Road in the spring. He passes a beautiful tree with other flowering vines entwined in it, glowing forth with a multitude of splendid colours. Whenever I see it, I think of love.

Another example from John's college is a small window that must be unique, hidden away in the chapel. It shows two figures only, Plato and Amos. They aren't looking at each other, but they are together nevertheless. That is a rarity in art, but it was the ideal of old Oxford to bring Hebrew and Greek thought together. Most of its art studies up to the 20th century focused on the Bible, Fathers of the Church, the Greek philosophers and poets. That was a heady combination where agape and eros had to inhabit a window together, even if they looked in different directions.

It is true that, without eros, we wouldn't have any society. But where would we be without agape as well as the other forms of love? Might we not run into a peck of trouble? Most would accept that we need to love ourselves, and have affection, friendship and loyalty toward town, job and nation. Many nations are worried that there might be breakdowns of societies without common values. Don't we need some heroes to fill out our societies? Don't we need these to demonstrate that life can be lived beyond, but including, mutual affection between lovers and self-giving love for friends and enemies? Where would we be today without Moses, Jesus, Mohammed, St. Teresa, St. Francis, Martin Luther King, Gandhi, et al?

Can we not mix these forms of love together, and create better relationships and society? Is it not possible to love God passionately, one's partner erotically, and still offer self-giving love for the poor? Cannot one form of love help the other? Might it even be possible to add one's country into the mix and have agape, eros, stergo and philia all running into each other? We can put ego into this collection along with the others, and apply all of them to God, the lover, one's country, generating a more exciting and wider love-up?

This is a fairly complex set of ideas. Let me pick them apart, and add a perspective from the biblical witnesses to make up a tasty recipe:

1. The first combination is eros and agape. There doesn't seem to be much of a problem in the Old Testament on this. It was simply assumed that you could love God mightily and one's partner(s) erotically. There is nary a hint that this wouldn't work, although the New Testament might not be so sure.
2. To this could be added the love (stergo) of Israel that all good Jews felt. Remember Jesus, weeping over this faithless lover, Jerusalem?
3. Along with this could be added the love (philia) Jesus had for the disciples and that most of them had for each other, an in-group with a close relationship but a sense of mission wider than themselves.
4. And to all of this could be added the self-love (ego) embodied in the rule, "Love your neighbour as you love yourself." The assumption was that you are able to love and not hate yourself, though this takes some work and doses of deep confession/acceptance/forgiveness or psychoanalysis (which often amounts to the same thing).

Taking another biblical example, one can develop Jesus and his various loves. Though the texts are notoriously difficult, I think we can show that he participated in a number of types of love. Agape was important

All You Need Is Love?

for him, and the chief example of the way he is alleged to have laid down his life for the sins of the world. Even though there are moments when he wanted to escape this burden, the biographers and interpreters wanted to state that it was, in the end, a willing sacrifice. This is one of humanity's supreme moments of love's expense.

It is difficult to analyse the relationship Jesus had with the disciples. It could be stormy and problematic, but seems also to be based on mutual affection and forgiveness. According to John, there was a favorite disciple, the one "whom Jesus loved" ("agape"and "philia" are used, but they were often interchangeable in the gospels, and one cannot make too much out of that). The point is that Jesus did make some distinctions between his close friends, loving some more personally than others.

There are not many references to family love, and there were obviously some troubles in the story as told in the Gospels when Jesus was irritated at his mother and brothers who were trying to speak with him. He is alleged to have said, "Who are my mother and brothers but those who do the will of God?" That was a put down, if there ever was one. But there are more tender examples of affection toward his mother, as in the account by John of the moment of his death when he commended his beloved disciple to his mother and his mother to him.

There are even fewer references in the bible to any erotic love Jesus may have harboured. Mary of Magdela is cited by the gnostic gospel quoted above, some novelists and the like, and many artists have drawn pictures of Jesus and Mary in the garden, expressing the words, "Do not touch me." But, unlike young men of his day, he did not marry, and any deep relationship with Mary of Magdela or any woman is not given in the texts. There was something going on, but we don't know what. What this example shows, I would assert, is that he was capable of a number of forms of love, including ego. There may not have been much in the way of erotic love from what we have to go on, but the rest seems rather well developed. The forms of love interpenetrated each other.

Love's Cure of Souls

Finally, I would also like to point out the interesting and relevant idea that John Wilson has made about love between equals helping to solve the problems of the dreadful perversions and aggressive behaviours that infect our world. He claims that mutual love between equals "may be an absolute necessity even for the limited objective of attaining some kind of decency or basic justice, for only in a context of such love can these forces (sex and aggression) be faced and deployed." (170)

He proceeds to say that if a person cannot act out or sublimate his/her aggressive and other feelings in bed or elsewhere with a loving partner, he/she will certainly act them out in some other more dangerous context. "The person must somehow get *his/her soul in order*" (author's italics, 170). Of course there must be rationally based moral principles that are taught to all of us, but that may not be enough, considering how prone to sexual perversions and aggressions human beings actually are. Most psychologists and many novelists have known for a long time the important connection between sex and violence.

It is interesting that Freud had something of the same notion in his method of psychoanalytic treatment. Patients acted out the repressed part of their relations with their parents or parent-figures that went wrong in childhood, and, in so doing, unloaded their love and hate onto the analyst as a parent figure who would carry their "sins" away by allowing himself to be scapegoated.

Freud said he was "in essence" (hauptasache) a Jew, but claimed it was up to the scientific community to define what this might mean. There are many theories on this, but my own theory is that "transference" is the clue. For that term, Freud had two uses. The first is that the analyst takes on the role of the parent or parent-figure that was loved and hated. The second is that the analyst draws onto himself or herself the love and hate that was reserved for the parent or parent-figure. I suggest this approach is a parallel to the scapegoat in Leviticus 16 where Aaron lays all the sins of Israel on the goat who bears them away, eventually to be taken into the wilderness or killed. As Anna Freud once said, without explaining herself, psychoanalysis is a "Jewish science." Perhaps that process is what she meant. It is a very ancient healing method.

Regarding John Wilson's intriguing point that Christianity foundered on the rocks of sin and aggression, it is significant to note that Genesis began with stories of sex and aggression (Adam/Eve; Cain/Abel). It might be that biblical ways of solving these problems have re-emerged in such shapers of the 20th century as the Freuds and Jungs. In any case, I would welcome into my set anybody, sacred or secular, to help solve these problems. It looks to me that we have much to gain from some of the Hebrew and Greek conceptions of love. I am grateful to John Wilson for helping me to see them more clearly, even if they are strange bedfellows, and even if he is rather suspicious of some of them.

Response to
the Contributors

Chapter Eight

A Personal Reply

John Wilson

It is immensely flattering to have a *Festschrift*, but also alarming. Perhaps the underlying thought is either (a) "This chap has plainly come to the end of this time; he's written out; it would be courteous to mark this by a *Festschrift,*" or (b) "This chap writes too much; perhaps a *Festschrift* will shut him up." Alas, neither (a) nor (b) is true. I hope to keep going for a bit longer.

I do not think I have done much, or perhaps any, work meriting the title of 'scholarly', except in ancient Greek history. Anyway, that is just a hobby. I hope, rather arrogantly, to have done some *good* work in philosophy; but for the kind of Socratic philosophy I admire and emulate, 'scholarly' does not seem a very relevant term of praise. 'Rigorous', yes; 'clear', certainly; 'imaginative' or 'challenging', perhaps; possibly even 'sane'. Philosophy is essentially a moral discipline, more like psychotherapy than anything else. Only too often I have not been rigorous enough, through impatience; sometimes not even sane. But at least I hope most of my work is clear, even if wrong.

Putting it pompously, the reason for these concerns is that I see myself as more of a missionary than a scholar. My chief interest is in the interface between philosophy and practical affairs. On the other hand, it is hard to survive the rigorous disciplines of College at Winchester and New College, Oxford, and even harder to face, and as it were, come out alive from the company of people like Jeremy Morse, Isaiah Berlin, Herbert Hart, Stuart Hampshire, Dick Hare and other worthies whose intelligence is several cuts above my own, without at least grasping the idea and importance of getting things right. Anything useful I have said or written (and I am frankly unsure what falls into this category), will have resulted partly from that discipline and partly from some sort of missionary zeal, no doubt psychologically suspect, which probably stems ultimately from being a parson's son. That accounts also for a somewhat chequered and not particularly distinguished career as a teacher and housemaster, a Professor of Religious Knowledge, a lecturer in philosophy, a director of a research unit, and now a resident philosopher in the Department of Educational Studies at Oxford.

The contributors refer, in far too kind a way, to the pleasure I take in intellectual discussion and conversation. It is true, I suppose, that I am usually a fairly popular figure in my work and social life, but sometimes I think this is in spite of, rather than because of, this predisposition. Some, I hope not too many, non-contributors would tell a different story. They would say, "Watch out for Wilson, he'll harass you and get at you and may well be 'offensive', certainly not politically correct." And there is some force in this warning. I have often been at least tactless, sometimes perhaps 'offensive' and objectionable, certainly not always behaving 'appropriately' in social terms. But it does raise an important question which holds public, not just personal, interest. How much onus (under this or that set of circumstances) should rest on A to be tactful and socially or politically correct, and how much onus on B not to be intolerant or paranoid? That is, I think, not just a question for the particular context of teaching and learning philosophy (see Rembert in Chapter One), but for social life and interpersonal relationships in general.

I myself (and this does have some public relevance) have always wanted to share myself as deeply and widely as possible with other people. (Doesn't everybody?) No doubt that accounts for my being what one might call a Compulsive Communicator. As the youngest child in a large family, I was (a) encouraged to deploy quite a lot of 'aggression' or at least forcefulness, to have a go at things, to join in and make a positive contribution; but also (b) to be friendly and kind, above all, not to hurt other people. Putting (a) and (b) together was a problem. (Isn't it for everybody?) I partly solved it by deploying my 'aggression' in institutional forms: I was the sort of odious child who not only came top in class, but was also captain of football and so forth. But a lot of the 'aggression' emerged, and still emerges, in intellectual discussion. I *mean well*, even when outrageous and politically incorrect, but my pleasure in this, or, if you like, the boredom or frustration of doing without it, is still not adequately controlled by tact. For that I can only apologise.

I offer these personal reflections because the philosopher or 'missionary', much like the psychotherapist, has to be secure enough within oneself to do a good job. Certain forms of intimate sharing are, I think, inevitably *painful*; and unless one party feels very secure, nothing will happen except bloodshed. I think there is a special onus on philosophers and teachers, in particular, to be secure: tact, patience and a genuine concern for the other, rather than just a compulsive desire to 'play', can only come from that, just as overcoming paranoia can only come from it. I take my lack of security here to be my greatest defect.

That is not by way of a confessional. I think much work remains to be done in this general field, especially relevant to educators. I think the amount of *wastage*, in education and personal relationships, that comes from difficulties of sharing the self securely is horrifying. In principle, at least, we all want to share, indeed sometimes desperately long to: we all want and need love in some form or other. But, in practice, it seems curiously difficult. Unless the basic problems here are stated clearly, more clearly than I have stated them, and solved, I doubt whether forms of sharing will be much more than ritualistic and superficial.

A cognate problem with public as well as private aspects is this: when does 'academic' or 'intellectual communication', or at least some kind of sophisticated conceptual interchange, help, and when doesn't it? Is this type of activity of any use? Is it possible to engage seriously and successfully in really intimate relationships or some public enterprises, like education or social work or church ministry, *without* trying to be both conceptually and psychologically clear? 'Philosophy' and 'psychotherapy' are only grand names for this. When Socrates says in Plato's *Apology* that *ho anexetastos bios abiotos anthropo,* "the unexamined life is not worth living (or, perhaps, 'not livable,') for human beings," does he mean that it is just nice or valuable or enriching to examine things, or that it is essential, if we are to avoid trouble?

Along with Plato, St. Augustine, Freud and others, I want to claim the latter: that human beings are in some kind of jam or problem situation, that not everything in the garden is lovely (even if/when we get 'society' right), that real happiness lies deep and has to be delved for. But maybe this is just me, not how it really is. And, of course, I quite see that there has to *be* a life *to* examine. Nevertheless there seems to be a real question here. Even if it were answered to my taste, there would still be no point (and some harm) in trying to *force* this on other people; but it might make some difference to one's practice all the same.

One comes back constantly here to the idea of intimate sharing, trust, security, openness and some kind of love or friendship. It is all very well for professional therapists: the clients come voluntarily, even paying for it. They are already motivated, the context of the consulting room is hived off from the rest of life. There are, of course, enormous difficulties and resistances, but they are part of the enterprise and recognised as such. But what about the rest of us? I once asked an eminent psychiatrist for tips on how to handle my students: he paused for about two minutes, looked me straight in the eye, and said, "It all depends on whether you yourself are a *real person*, John." That more or less finished me off completely; I went away and resolved to get a bit more real everyday, until finally I might actually find myself existing. . . . No, but these questions are serious. In this brief space, I can only outline them and commend them to other people more able than myself.

Now to business. I shall be fairly brief about this too because what the contributors, perhaps too kindly have written cannot be justly addressed except at very great length, which is inappropriate here. What I can do, which may be of some use and interest, is to try to highlight the crucial points of *disagreement* as I see them. Of course, I have the unfair advantage that they cannot respond.

A Personal Reply

Response to the Essays of the Contributors

Chapter One "Plato's Images Describing Discussants That Act Up and Discussions That Break Down," by Ron Rembert

For years, I have failed to incite Ron Rembert to violence despite my best efforts, and there are no points in his article at which we disagree with each other. Ron is one of the curiously few philosophers who have a deep interest in how to get their discipline across (why are there so few?); and I think he is right to focus on Plato and/or Socrates, who is one of the few.

Where we *might* disagree is on this question, which is an important one in itself: how, in philosophical discussion or before it, should we handle basic psychological or psychiatric issues marked by terms like 'aggression', 'paranoia', or 'transference'? What actually *happens* in the Socratic dialogues, particularly in the *locus classicus* of Book I of the *Republic,* clearly turns on the participants' attitude to their 'positive or negative transference' on Socrates himself. That attitude underlies and dictates what they say and the way they participate. Here I should want to say, as perhaps Ron might not, (a) that the participants should be aware of these basic concepts and their application to themselves, in something like the way in which participants in group psychotherapy are made aware of this; and (b) perhaps more controversially, that unless some form of 'aggression', or some kind of forceful and weight-carrying investment, is actually brought into the discussion, then the discussion will become ritualised, bland, and too eirenic. To put it rather ferociously: we cannot *both* follow the conventional norms of social harmony and reinforcement *and* do philosophy seriously, at least not at the same time. As indeed sometimes in everyday life, the norms conflict. One cannot always satisfy the demands both of truth and of benevolence.

There is a connected question of how much philosophy (or, come to that, psychotherapy or education)

anyone can *stand*. Perhaps none of us can stand very much because it is too painful. It is very important to be clear when one is engaged in one form of life or another, for instance whether we are reinforcing our identities, or making each other feel good, or seriously pursuing truth. Of course, in principle, these can be combined, if we already have people who find pleasure and reinforcement *in* pursuing truth. But that is rare: for practical reasons we need to distinguish these forms of life, clarify them, and agree about when, where, and for how long we are going to engage in them.

Chapter Two "The Basis of Moral Education," by Samuel M. Natale, William O'Neill and Joanne C. Neher

I supervised Sam Natale's doctoral thesis at Oxford some twenty years ago, and it is delightful to see that the issues we then discussed are still alive. With the psychological and empirical background in the article I do not disagree. Indeed I am not psychologically qualified to agree or disagree. But with one central point of what may be called the philosophical underpinning, I strongly disagree; that is, assuming that I understand it properly.

At the very beginning of the article the authors say: "Moral education can, and certainly should, rest on reason and logic." It seems that it mustn't rest on the Bible or the Koran or Karl Marx or some other supposedly authoritative picture or ideal. The authors continue: "That, however, does not necessarily entail that having particular *moral content, even at the start* [my italics] conflicts with a foundation in reason and logic." This might mean (a) that in the actual practice of moral education children need to be taught some particular moral content, perhaps even when they are young, to be regarded as authoritative and unquestionable. That is harmless and indeed necessary, in fact inevitable, not just because they have to be 'socialized', but because they would not know what a moral principle *was* unless they were given some. But it might mean (b) that the moral educators

A Personal Reply 119

themselves, *qua* moral educators, might take some moral content (the Bible or whatever) as the *basis* of what they do: that they might see it as their task, 'at the start', to transmit or inculcate that content.

The same ambiguity arises when the authors say later: "The question remains as to whether this reasoning [*sc.* 'sound moral reasoning'] can be global... Any framework is culture-bound. Therefore, any moral decisions affecting education or behavior must be tested and questioned within that culture." That might mean (a) that armed with (culture-free) knowledge of how to reason morally, i.e., being competent within the *form* of morality rather than inculcated with a particular moral *content*, we must then in our moral decisions take into account the empirical facts of this or that culture or, indeed, any other relevant cultural facts. Of course that is true. But it might mean (b) that there can be *no* culture-free, as it were transcendental, 'framework' provided by pure reason which shows us *how* to get right moral answers (not *what* answers which will depend partly on the facts). Such a framework would also show us which facts are *relevant*.

Perhaps I do the authors an injustice here. In any case, I have tried to explain at length elsewhere (Wilson, 1990) why (b) will not do, and I shall not bore the reader here by repeating it. The point is worth raising because I believe the chief barrier to progress in moral education is, in fact, the immense temptation to rely 'at the start' on some particular moral content, as if we felt that we had to inject our children with *some* such content and worry only about that with which we fill the syringes.

Chapter Three "The Context of Moral Education: The Virtues of a Learning Community," by Felicity Fletcher-Campbell

It is difficult to disagree with Felicity Fletcher-Campbell's extremely thoughtful article which is much too kind to me personally. I am not much worried by that fact that my original contribution now seems 'dated' (it was written in 1972), or that "the model advocated by

Wilson seems increasingly nebulous and inviable within the present context of education." No doubt what we write in the 1990s will seem so in a few decades. Perhaps, though, I should have made more mention of other institutions of which I have had some experience, not just College at Winchester, but the kibbutzim, the army, an extended family, state boarding schools, some African tribes. . . .

I heartily agree with her main point (first, I think, explicitly made by Plato in the *Republic*): "The intellectual virtues are themselves 'moral' and can serve moral education," together with what she draws and clarifies from Telfer and Sockett about honesty, perseverance, carefulness, courage, heed and control. On any account there will be virtues which apply to *any* kind of serious learning or education. Where I might disagree is with the idea that the "availability" of "potent relationships" . . . "can be established within more conventional setups . . . their quintessence is implied in the very activity of teaching, *rather than* in any particular social arrangement." (my italics)

This is because the fundamental conceptual constituent of education is learning, not teaching. Many things have to be taught, and may best be taught in a traditional classroom, although that may be more questionable than we think. Much learning is more or less *picked up* in the family without much or any overt teaching. And, if we think of the school as 'a learning community', it is not at all clear that, for instance, the learning of languages or literary appreciation or music is best done, or only done, by classroom teaching. When we think of social relationships, religious or political learning, or moral education, it becomes much less clear (a) what part is played by overt teaching (in the classroom or elsewhere) which is an important part, and (b) what part is better played in other contexts and by other methods. That is also a question for the family: how much should the parents *teach* morality, and how much should they rather initiate and share various practices and forms of life with their children? None of this reneges on Fletcher-Campbell's point that, whatever learning goes on, the pupils need to cultivate the intellectual virtues. Some of this turns, however, on what we are going to count as 'teaching'.

My claim is (and it would take a lot of both conceptual and empirical argument to make it good) that quite a lot of moral education needs contexts and communities much more 'potent', much more like an extended family, than most schools provide today. So I think that 'particular social arrangements', the social *structure* of the school, are very important, and that appropriate ones are sadly lacking. That is why most older pupils get most of their moral or social 'education' from their peer groups and even from the street gangs. Of course 'potent' communities have their problems as the recent history of the kibbutzim shows, particularly for those who are not by nature 'communal.' They can be very oppressive and destructive of individuality and privacy. Nevertheless children and adolescents do *need* 'potency' and communality, if only to get the love and support that their families may have denied them; so that we have the gigantic task of working out just what kind of communities suit what kinds (ages, sexes, psychological types) of pupils.

Nevertheless she is absolutely right to insist on the centrality of l*earning*: it is not just that we want to give everybody a good time and a chance to make friends, nor that we want to make pupils merely the *recipients* of benefits under the heading of 'pastoral care' or whatever. They are *responsible agents:* the chief point about education is that it is something people *do*, namely learn, not something *given* to them, like money or cake. It is, I suspect, failure to appreciate this point that inhibits us from even thinking about how a 'potent' school community should look. In all serious communities, from football teams and orchestras to the kibbutzim and the family, individuals are not just 'cared for' as recipients: they are given responsibilities and tasks, sometimes quite tough ones. There is much more to say about the underlying attitudes and fantasies which, in the current climate, make us miss this point. But I shall not say it here.

Chapter Four "The Public School Model" by Henry Near

I have never known quite how to deal with Henry Near, another old and, like the rest of us, aging friend. His article is a mixture of history and social psychology or sociology, rising at times to the giddy heights of philosophy. I found it extremely illuminating, and again difficult to find points of disagreement on any substantive issues.

A trivial issue may be turned into a substantive one or at least a methodological one. What he says about the "ideal public school man" and "the results of public school education" ("overwhelmingly to produce conformist upper-class citizens") seems questionable. And when he mentions the essential characteristics—"esprit de corps, patriotism, a willingness to take on public service"—I thought, before I read the text more carefully, that he was talking about kibbutzniks. My point is simply that if we are to grasp problems about communities, their particular parochial qualities may often be irrelevant. The kibbutzim, like Winchester College, are a special case. Many of the basic features of any close-knit community are to be found outside detribalized communities, in more or less any tribe. That certain recent or contemporary communities may be based on well-articulated ideologies may be, if I have the term right, just an epiphenomenon, not central to the main issues.

On one central issue I disagree: "The social function of any school must be . . . to promote the values and ideals of the society which affords it legal and social legitimation" (there speaks the sociologist). Of course I see the point; but if that *had* always to be true, then any serious political education would be impossible, for there

A Personal Reply 123

would be no significant arena in which the students could question these values and ideals. That is important, because if any community is to allow the kind of change necessary for survival, perhaps, it must not only allow but encourage such an arena. The history of many communities, perhaps even of the kibbutzim, commonly shows a kind of *ossification,* whereby changing conditions or climates of opinion, or merely the coming of a new generation, may marginalise the community or even destroy it.

The questions Near rightly raises cannot, in principle, be settled by ideological or other intuitions. They include questions about what types of people are psychologically best suited by what types of community (what degree of privacy as against communality is required, for instance); in particular, perhaps, about the place of the family, or the necessity or non-necessity of the community being economically self-sufficient. And such questions are greatly complicated by the facts (a) that the way in which children are brought up within the community itself influences their psychology and hence their subsequent choices, and, even worse, (b) that one may *think* oneself suited by this or that set-up, but *be wrong*. (Thus, characteristically, there will be a temptation to opt out of communal life and set up one's own, with as high degree of independence and as high a standard of living as one can get; whether people who do this are any *happier* is another question.)

Thus, being a lonely philosopher, my heart warms when Near talks of 'communion', but such talk, even when not overtly metaphysical, at once raises the question of what *sort* of communion people need. Should I just make more friends? Or spend more time in communal tasks with my colleagues? Join a football team? Seek for an ideal soul-mate in the opposite sex? Or just stick to a scholar's life ("Books are my friends")? These are serious questions. We need, *without* the benefit of partisan ideology, to get some sort of adequate picture of what kind of relationships people are suited for, and that can hardly be done without the benefit of post-Freudian psychology, what I take to be the most important discipline here. Even then it will be difficult, because our attitude towards and desire for certain types of relationships is learned in early childhood, so that people will vary. Worse still, people will grow out of some of these variations while not growing out of others, and we will have trouble in adjudicating which will and which will not.

All of this is somewhat depressing, but we just have to work harder. What Near here and elsewhere (see his references) says about the kibbutzim is immensely interesting, chiefly because we have in them ongoing communities with a history and a set of problems that have been *monitored* by highly intelligent people like, to throw a bouquet, Near. But, swiftly retracting this compliment, it is important that such people are not *so* committed to particular types of communities that they do not probe deeper into the problems which can and should be generalised, if only because the particular communities themselves will suffer if they are not solved.

Chapter Five "Being a Bit Pregnant: How Philosophical Misconceptions Lead to Stillborn Empirical Research" by Robin Barrow

Robin Barrow agrees with me, or I with him, too much for me to do justice to his illuminating paper which contains many points of great importance. However, there is one absolutely crucial point about which perhaps both of us are unclear.

Note the following: "One of the points about which Wilson and I disagree is whether it makes sense to say that a given conception is true, whether, for example, one can talk about the true meaning of 'education' . . . I believe that the notion of a true conception is meaningless." That is going to turn on what we mean by 'concept' and 'conception'. If (a) we mean by either of

A Personal Reply

these words anything like 'idea', 'picture' or 'understanding', then a concept/conception can be a personal possession. We may talk of my or your or his concept, for example, "His conception of education is . . .". Then, of course, Barrow is right because 'a true conception' is now meaningless: a conception might be a bit thin, or peculiar, or comforting, or dictated by some set of power-holders, or prevalent in the twentieth century climate or whatever. But if (b) by 'concept' we mean something like 'a range of meaning as marked perhaps, but perhaps not, by the term "x" in late twentieth-century English', it is another matter. Terms mark what they mark. They are public, not private entities. In that sense, we may speak of 'the concept', and people are either clear in their minds about it or they are not.

I hope (because some interesting blood would flow) that Barrow disagrees with the notion that philosophy, as against some kind of high-level sociology or the history of ideas, should be confined to (b) rather than (a). The philosopher is concerned with culture-free, transcendental distinctions. These *may* be marked in this or that language, but they may not; it may be, as Austin puts it, as much a matter of "making clear distinctions rather than making existing distinctions clear." We *start* perhaps with terms in natural language. Where else could we start? They mark some, indeed many, important distinctions; but the distinctions are, as it were, *there*, *available* and teachable, whether they are so marked or not.

This is the best I can do by way of disagreement. There are, of course, other issues I should like to take up, perhaps particularly the way in which Barrow speaks blithely of 'quantitative' and 'qualitative' research, as if we know what these terms mean. I do not, despite (or maybe because of) having read books about them. (For example, She loves me *du tout, un peu, beaucoup, passionement, a la folie*; is that 'qualitative' or is it 'quantitative'?) I suspect my views on educational research are more philosophically radical even than Barrow's. I think we really have *no idea* how to do such research, or even what it is, and had better start from scratch. A rational concept, or conception, of educational research would, I am sure, look quite different from the demoralised and extremely boring cultural phenomenon that now is marked by that phrase.

Chapter Six   "John Wilson and the Basis of Education," by Spencer Maxcy

Spencer Maxcy is again much too kind, and again I have to agree with much of what he says. However, there is perhaps one difference which stands between us: a difference of methodology or heuristics rather than of substance, but all the more important for that.

Maxcy rightly takes me to task for advocating or, at least, for appearing to advocate, a certain substantive position, perhaps even an 'ideology': my "conception of education rests on four fundamental ideas: reason, rule-authority, leadership and morality." That is my fault, and not his; but I wonder whether he would agree with me that the philosopher, *qua* philosopher, has no business to be advocating substantive positions at all. For any such positions, particularly in politics and education, must rely on empirical facts, which the philosopher as such is not qualified to deploy.

As a philosopher rather than an ideologue, I should have to try to show (I shall not re-attempt it here), that certain concepts had to be attended to *whatever* the empirical facts, and whatever our individual preferences, might be. For instance, the concepts normally marked by 'authority', 'social rules', 'sanctions' and so on are not, I would argue, *optional*. We could not have anything like a *society* without using and applying them. So too with 'reason', 'leadership', and 'morality'; these concepts are necessarily written into all forms of human life. The philosopher's job is to clarify them fully, connect them with each other, and show their inevitability. It is not his job to advocate any particular ideology or political system.

A Personal Reply

That point emerges if we consider the concept that might be marked by 'liberal' or 'liberalism'. These terms may be, perhaps most commonly are, used (a) to refer to a particular substantive political position, in which, I suppose, freedom is maximised, tolerance is a prime virtue, individualism is encouraged, and so on. Here, whether or not one ought to be 'a liberal' will obviously depend largely on empirical facts, on the particular society one is considering. But they might also (b) point one in the direction of certain logical or conceptual or necessary truths: perhaps, for instance, towards the notion of universalisability in making value-judgments (in effect, the Golden Rule as deployed by Kant and, in our own day, R.M. Hare). That is a quite different business; there is nothing empirical or sociological or ideological about it *at all*.

Sound political decisions (and the same applies to morality, education and most other enterprises) are a matter of (1) getting the relevant concepts clear, which is the philosopher's job, and (2) assembling the relevant empirical facts, which is not. We need both, I think, in that order. But nothing is to be gained by confusing (1) with (2), and there is no respectable 'third world' of theory or ideology. *Concepts* and *facts* are all we have. That is quite enough.

Chapter Seven "All You Need Is Love?" by Charles Brock

It is peculiarly difficult to find disagreement with Charles Brock's article, chiefly because, like Charles, it is so disarming.

Perhaps his most disarming and interesting proposal emerges when he talks of "Analyses by Wilson and Freud," a flattering but undeserved comparison helping us to see these problems: "if *agape* is used as the one and only allowable form of love or, if misunderstood, is the cause of cold, truncated, amputated, dutiful detachment that is such a frost." Then he says, "Why not add *agape,* but mix it with the others [*sc.* other kinds of love] so that we have a fizzier cocktail?" That is an appealing proposition, at least to those of us, like myself, who have been brought up on *agape* and think that no family can afford to be without some of it. On this view, if suitably elaborated, we need not *choose between agape* and what I have described under the heading of 'love between equals' (a mixture of *eros* and *philia*). We may unite them, perhaps seeing some kinds of love as *forms* of *agape* or else we may practise both side by side.

My doubts are twofold. First, I want to be loved as an equal and not as a client or protégé, *de haut en bas*, however altruistically. If *agape* had the idea of equality built into it (perhaps it has or could have), all would be well. Second, I want to be loved as an individual, in my deepest self, not only strongly (*agape* may be very strong) but, for want of a better word, erotically. That, of course, does not mean, or only mean, that I want to go to bed with somebody; it means rather that the deep part of myself, which normally I reserve from others including my closest friends or members of my family, has to love and be loved. It involves not only 'sex', but also very basic feelings about power, independence, and justice. I have to share and negotiate those on an equal basis with my partner; and that, as we all know, is a very different matter. If *agape* is to include that, I have no quarrel; but, as the ideal is usually employed, it does not.

Brock's quotations of "advice to maintain a good marriage" are relevant here: "Romance and passion are less important than mutual goodwill," "Compromise," "Stick to the point in rows and don't character-assassinate," "Talk about what you value in each other," "Don't cheat." These are typical. But, one might ask, why should I *bother* to go in for this somewhat arduous process of deploying constant *agape* when living cheek by jowl with another person, bound at least notionally for life, probably with substantially different tastes and life-style from myself, *unless I love her/him?* So there must be more to this kind of love than *agape,* or at least the kind of *agape* which the advice columns propagate, and quite rightly propagate, if what we want to do is to keep an existing relationship or family ship afloat.

It is somewhat like other tips in the advice column on how to "spice up your sex life." If I really love my partner, I see him/her as the most desirable or beautiful or exciting person in the world, to me anyway. I do not really need tips to spice up my sex life, it is already spiced. And if I do not love him/her, if I do not see him/her in this sort of light, then no amount of spice will do the job: it will rather produce a sort of empty caricature or parody of love, or a desperate and doomed attempt to recapture it, if it was ever there. There is a reasonably clear distinction between a *mariage d'amour* and a *mariage de convenance*, as between Aristotle's intrinsic and extrinsic friendships. (*Nicomachean Ethics*.) To put it summarily, either I am hooked on the other person who really has my heart, my deepest feelings and passion or I am not so hooked. Of course, everyone really *wants* to be hooked or bonded in that way for life, to have a passionate lover, 'another self' (Aristotle's *allos autos*), who loves and is loved idiosyncratically, uniquely, and at that deep level of the self. But it is difficult, and many people despair of it.

None of that implies that *agape* can be dispensed with. Certainly it is, as Brock says, essential for almost any serious form of life, of universal application and importance. Not many people seem very *good* at it. I think that is chiefly because (here Brock agrees) they do not face their own aggression and eroticism, which then emerge in uncontrolled forms and cause disaster or, at least, the "frost" about which Brock speaks. Even in the closest personal relationships, the principle, habit and practice of treating the other as an equal and with benevolence are vital, though the motivation will be different, a delight and not, or as well as, a duty. The chief thing to be said in favour of *agape* is that it is *indispensable* so long as we relate to other people at all. In addition, it may also enter into the important notion of loving ourselves. Love between equals, as I have described it, is in this sense dispensable, that we can live decent lives without it, I mean, lives that are perfectly respectable and even of some use to others. But it is, I believe, a form of life which all people badly need. And I agree with Trollope, hardly the most 'romantic' of authors who nevertheless says at the end of one of his novels, that the person who does not go in for it will have a life which is "small, and poor, and dry."

*****

Finally, I should like, quite seriously (I *can* be serious sometimes) to express my thanks both to Ron Rembert for initiating this project and spending so much trouble on it, and also to all the contributors for also giving time and effort which *sub specie aeternitatis* might have been better spent elsewhere. I certainly do not *deserve* a *Festschrift*, but then I do not deserve most of the nice things I have had and continue to have in my life. Whilst expressing my gratitude for these contributors making it at least *look* as if I had something useful to say, I can only hope that what they themselves say in this book, and perhaps even my comments on it, will be of some general interest, and not just a reinforcement to my ego.